How to Use This Book

The Scribner Essentials for Writers is a quick reference work to consult about matters of grammar, punctuation, mechanics, style, and research. Here's how to find what you're looking for.

Front endpapers: The compact content chart provides an overview of the section and page numbers of key topics you will need.

Main contents: A detailed listing of sections and page numbers for all topics appears on the inside back cover.

Index: This alphabetical list of topics, words, and terms begins on page 175.

Directory to Documentation models: Directories for citation and bibliographic models appear in the sections for each documentation style: MLA (pp. 30–47); APA (pp. 48–62). Guidelines for using CMS and CBE styles are also included.

Glossaries: The glossary of usage (p. 159) helps you use words and expressions correctly, such as *affect* and *effect*. The glossary of grammatical terms provides definitions of key terms and cross-references to related coverage in the book.

Use the elements of the page. These include:

- Page tabs indicating part and section number
- Running heads and page numbers
- Bold type identifying key terms
- Cross-references providing section numbers of related topics
- Examples illustrating instructional points

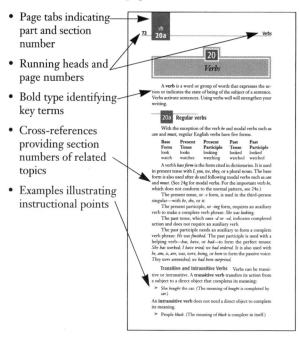

72

vb
20a

Verbs

20
Verbs

A **verb** is a word or group of words that expresses the action or indicates the state of being of the subject of a sentence. Verbs activate sentences. Using verbs well will strengthen your writing.

20a Regular verbs

With the exception of the verb *be* and modal verbs such as *can* and *must*, regular English verbs have five forms.

Base Form	Present Tense	Present Participle	Past Tense	Past Participle
look	looks	looking	looked	looked
watch	watches	watching	watched	watched

A verb's *base form* is the form cited in dictionaries. It is used in present tense with *I, you, we, they,* or a plural noun. The base form is also used after *do* and following modal verbs such as *can* and *must*. (See 24g for modal verbs. For the important verb *be,* which does not conform to the normal pattern, see 24e.)

The present tense, or *-s* form, is used in the third-person singular—with *he, she,* or *it.*

The present participle, or *-ing* form, requires an auxiliary verb to make a complete verb phrase: *She was looking.*

The past tense, which uses *-d* or *-ed,* indicates completed action and does not require an auxiliary verb.

The past participle needs an auxiliary to form a complete verb phrase: *He was finished.* The past participle is used with a helping verb—*has, have,* or *had*—to form the perfect tenses: *She has worked; I have tried; we had ordered.* It is also used with *be, am, is, are, was, were, being,* or *been* to form the passive voice: *They were astonished; we had been surprised.*

Transitive and Intransitive Verbs   Verbs can be transitive or intransitive. A **transitive verb** transfers its action from a subject to a direct object that completes its meaning:

➤ She *bought* the car. (The meaning of *bought* is completed by *car.*)

An **intransitive verb** does not need a direct object to complete its meaning.

➤ People *blush.* (The meaning of *blush* is complete in itself.)

The Scribner Essentials for Writers

Robert DiYanni
Pace University

Pat C. Hoy II
New York University

ALLYN AND BACON

Boston London Toronto Sydney Tokyo Singapore

Vice President and Editor in Chief, Humanities: *Joseph Opiela*
Senior Development Editor: *Ellen Darion*
Series Editorial Assistant: *Julie Hallett*
Marketing Manager: *Christopher Bennem*
Composition and Prepress Buyer: *Linda Cox*
Cover Administrator: *Linda Knowles*
Production Administrator: *Susan Brown*
Editorial-Production Service: *Kathy Smith*
Text Designer: *Carol Somberg/Omegatype Typography, Inc.*
Electronic Composition: *Omegatype Typography, Inc.*

Copyright © 2001 by Allyn & Bacon
A Pearson Education Company
Needham Heights, MA 02494

Internet: www.abacon.com

Between the time Website information is gathered and then published, it is not unusual for some sites to have closed. Also, the transcription of URLs can result in unintended typographical errors. The publisher would appreciate notification where these occur so that they may be corrected in subsequent editions.

Library of Congress Cataloging-in-Publication Data

DiYanni, Robert.
    The Scribner essentials for writers / Robert DiYanni, Patrick C. Hoy II.
        p.   cm.
    Includes index.
    ISBN 0-205-31903-3
    1. English language—Rhetoric—Handbooks, manuals, etc.
    2. English language—Grammar—Handbooks, manuals, etc.
    3. Report writing—Handbooks, manuals, etc. I. Title: Essentials for writers. II. Hoy, Pat C. III. Title.

PE1408.D588 2000
808'.042—dc21   00-060588

Printed in the United States of America
10 9 8 7 6 5 4 3 2 1   04   03   02   01   00

The Writing, Reading, and Thinking Connection

1

Writing, Reading, and Thinking

Reading helps you acquire and consider *ideas* for writing. As you accumulate knowledge and learn what you want to say and how to say it, writing becomes its own reward. Your *audience* begins to understand what you have on your mind, and, if you are persuasive, your readers may even begin to see things your way.

As you learn to read critically and write reflectively, you will learn to think creatively and logically about what others have written. Initially, you will be influenced by the ideas you discover as you read. Creative thinking helps you recognize those ideas (just as it will help you, eventually, to generate ideas of your own); logical thinking helps you analyze and evaluate those ideas. That creative process of evaluation and reflection leads you to your own ideas, which, eventually, provide the foundation for your essays.

As you begin to develop your essays, the evidence that you select from your various sources provides the basis for your readers' understanding and acceptance of your ideas. Each essay that you write will be based on an idea you have discovered—the leading thought (often called a *thesis*) that you are trying to convey to your readers. Your selected evidence, gathered through reading and research, will give substance to that idea while making your written work clearer and more convincing.

The reading you do in college most often is critical reading; it requires careful analysis and thoughtful response. The word *critical* in this approach to reading does not mean "being critical of" in the familiar sense of disapproval. **Critical reading** involves reacting to what you read, analyzing it, interpreting it, and evaluating its ideas and assessing its values.

2

Writing from Reading

You can expect much of your college reading to lead to writing assignments such as essays, research papers, and reports.

To develop those assignments, react to what you read by making marginal notes or annotations (only if you own the text, of course). Afterward, do some reflective writing, such as freewriting. Keep a double-column notebook or a reading journal, or write a summary. The kind of writing you do will be determined by your purpose.

2a Reacting to a text with annotations

Annotations are brief notes you write about a text while reading it. Underline and circle words and phrases that strike you as important. Make marginal comments that reflect your attitude toward the text. Include arrows that identify related points, question marks that indicate your confusion, and exclamation marks to express your surprise. Depending on how extensively you annotate a text, your annotations may form a secondary text that reminds you of the text you are reading. Annotations used this way serve as an abbreviated outline of what the text says and of what you think about it.

2b Reflecting on a text in freewriting

Your initial impressions of a text, which you can record with annotations, will often lead you to further thoughts about it. You can develop these thoughts with **freewriting**, an invention technique that serves as a source of ideas for writing. In freewriting, you record your ideas, reactions, or feelings about a text without arranging them in any special order. You simply write down what you think about the passage, without worrying about spelling or grammar. Freewriting, in fact, offers you a way to pursue an idea, to develop your thinking to see where it may lead.

2c Using a double-column notebook

To create a **double-column notebook**, simply divide your page in half. One half is for summarizing and interpreting what you read. Use this side of the page to record as accurately as you can your understanding of what the text says. Use the other side to respond to what you have read, think about its implications, and relate it to other things you have read or otherwise experienced.

The advantage of a double-column notebook is that it encourages you to be an active reader, to think about what you read, and to make connections with your reading and experience rather than to consider a text in isolation. You can use the double-column notebook to think further about your earlier reactions, which you may have recorded in annotations or freewriting, and to sustain conversations with both the writer and yourself.

2d Writing a summary

Summarize a text when you need to give your readers the gist of what it says. A **summary** should present the author's text accurately and represent his or her views fairly. Build your summary on the observations, connections, and inferences you make while reading. A summary is always shorter than the text itself.

Writing a summary requires careful reading, in part to assure that you understand a text well. Writing a summary helps you respond to a text by requiring you to analyze and consider its details. Your goal in summarizing a text is to render a writer's ideas accurately and fairly.

One strategy for writing a summary is to find the key points that support the main idea. You can do this by looking for clusters of sentences or groups of paragraphs that convey the writer's meaning. Because paragraphs work together, you cannot simply summarize each paragraph independently. You may need to summarize a cluster of paragraphs to convey the idea of a text effectively. (For more on paraphrase and summary, see Chapter 15.)

3

Analyzing What You Read

After reacting to a text with annotations, reflecting on it in freewriting, and perhaps summarizing it or recording your thoughts about it in a double-column notebook, you can return to it for further analysis. When you **analyze** a text, you isolate and look closely at its parts (the beginning, middle, and ending of an essay or article, for example, or the sequence of events in a story). Focus on one element at a time, observing its details. Then look for connections and relationships among those details. Your goal in analyzing a text is to understand it, to see how its parts fit together to make sense as a whole.

3a Observing details

The kinds of observations you make about a text will depend upon the kind of text you are reading. If you are reading a scientific report, you will observe its argument and the evidence that supports it. If you are reading a psychological abstract, you will attend to the purpose and limits of the study as well to the kind of field research it may involve. In reading literary works, you will consider such elements as diction and imagery, character and conflict, and style and structure. Your instructor may also encourage you to focus on particular features of a text.

3b Connecting the details

It is not enough simply to observe details about a text. You must also connect them with one another. To make a connection is to see one thing in relation to another. You may notice that some details reinforce others, or that the writer repeats certain words. Perhaps the writer sets up a contrast.

While you are noticing aspects of a text, you can also begin making connections among its details. Your goal is to see how the connected details help you make sense of the text as a whole. This involves setting up categories or headings for related details.

Making observations about a text and establishing connections among them form the basis of analysis. From that basis you begin to consider the significance of what you observe and proceed to develop an interpretation.

4

Formulating an Interpretation

An **interpretation** is your tentative or provisional conclusion about a text based on your analysis of it (your observations and connections). To arrive at an interpretation, you need to make inferences based on your observations. An **inference** is a statement you make based on what you have observed. You infer a writer's idea or point of view, for instance, from the examples and evidence he or she provides. Inferences drive the interpretive process. They push you beyond making observations toward explaining them and the text.

4a Making inferences

You make inferences in everyday life all the time, and there is nothing mysterious about the process. If you see someone at

8 a.m. with a large ring of keys opening a classroom door in a university building, you may infer that he or she is a member of the school staff whose job it is to unlock classroom doors. Of course, you may be right or wrong about your inference, but you will have made a reasonable inference nonetheless.

The same is true when you make inferences about a text. Your inference provides a way of understanding a text by "reading between the lines," by discovering what is implied rather than explicitly stated.

Remember that an inference can be right or wrong, and thus different readers might debate the reliability of these or other inferences. The important thing is not to be afraid to make an inference because you think a particular inference might be challenged or questioned. Critical reading involves thinking. Thinking involves making inferences. Making inferences and thinking about what you read help you arrive at an interpretation of the text.

4b Arriving at an interpretation

The step from drawing inferences to arriving at an interpretation is small. An interpretation is a way of explaining the meaning of a text; it represents your way of understanding the text expressed as an idea.

Your goal in interpreting any text is to understand it so that you can explain its meaning accurately. Informative texts, such as newspaper reports about current events or textbook material about scientific processes, require factual understanding and accuracy. Literary texts demand accurate observations and defensible inferences. Persuasive interpretations are characterized by these qualities.

When you arrive at an interpretation, look back at the text's details to reconsider your initial observations as well as to review the connections you established to see if they still make sense. Consider whether your inferences are defensible—that is, whether you can offer support on their behalf. Look also to see if additional details can support your inferences, or whether you wish to make different inferences that may lead to another interpretation.

You may decide later to interpret the text differently. You arrive at your idea about the text's meaning by reaching a conclusion based on your inferences. These inferences, in turn, are based on your observations about the text and the connections you make among those observations.

5

Using Logical and Creative Thinking Together

The kind of logical, inferential thinking that leads to sound interpretations of texts is most often accompanied by creative thinking. Both logical and creative thinking are necessary for writing. Creative thinking helps you evaluate ideas and evidence that emerge in reading, in discussion, and in your own writing. These two kinds of thinking complement and reinforce one another. The accompanying chart clarifies the major features of both creative and logical thinking.

Overview of Creative and Logical Thinking

- Creative thinking puts things together; it synthesizes.
- Logical thinking analyzes things; it takes them apart.

- Creative thinking generates new ideas.
- Logical thinking evaluates previously formulated ideas.

- Creative thinking explores many alternatives.
- Logical thinking focuses on finding an answer and being correct at each step.

- Creative thinking is inclusive, admitting all ideas.
- Logical thinking is selective, screening out bad ideas.

- Creative thinking is random. It permits jumps beyond the next step in a logical sequence.
- Logical thinking is linear and sequential. It moves from point to point in a straight line, allowing for no skips or gaps.

- Creative thinking forestalls judgment; it deliberately delays critical evaluation.
- Logical thinking encourages making judgments; it assesses whether an idea or piece of evidence is valid.

- Creative thinking is questioning, tentative, provisional.
- Logical thinking is more assertive, confident.

6

Discovering and Developing Ideas

The development of your own ideas is closely related to your ability to identify ideas in the texts that you read and evaluate. Ideas do not usually come to us out of the blue; they come instead on the heels of reading and observing and thinking about the information that we accumulate through a process of *researching*. Developing ideas is always an interesting process because ideas are never fixed; they are elastic. They are, as one student said, "Always capable of further analysis."

Ideas come from a variety of sources: your reading, your consideration of a painting or a photograph, your own experiences, a movie or play that you have seen. They take shape as your mind plays over such sources and begins to make sense of them.

The following techniques can help you formulate and develop ideas:

- Considering controversies
- Questioning
- Writing
- Connecting
- Collaborating

These five techniques should help you as you move *from* evidence *to* ideas *to* essays. The techniques are highly effective when you use them concurrently. We begin with controversy because it is so closely aligned with much of the academic writing that you will do, but we could just as easily begin with one of the other techniques.

6a   Finding an idea within controversies

Typically, when doing assigned research, you will be asked to develop a leading idea in the form of a thesis—your point of view about your subject, your conclusion about what the evidence means. One effective way to discover your own point of view is to consider what others have written about your subject. Differing points of view signal a topic worthy of your consideration; they point to the heart of the controversy.

For every controversial issue, you are sure to find special-interest groups that insist on your seeing the issue the way they do. First, broaden your understanding through research. Next, sort out the issues, making sure not to overlook important information and evidence. Finally, try to resolve the controversy: modify your conclusion in light of the evidence and formulate your thesis.

6b Questioning evidence to find an idea

Questioning evidence accompanies every effort to develop an idea. Questioning follows from a natural human curiosity about what something means. Writing about the evidence even before you have developed your idea often leads to more questions and helps you clarify what the evidence means (see 6c). As you write, your mind reaches back into memory or leaps from one piece of evidence to another, making connections, helping you discover meaning.

The following steps will help you look for patterns and meaning in the evidence you evaluate. That evidence could be a written text, a painting, or a photograph—anything that is related to your area of inquiry.

1. Begin with evidence that interests you.

2. Study it, trying to understand what it means. Consider these questions:
   a. What do I first notice about the evidence?
   b. How do I feel about what I am reading?
   c. Are any patterns obvious in the evidence?
   d. When I look again, do I realize some deeper meaning that was not so obvious on first consideration? What can I infer logically from the evidence?

3. Think about the evidence and the assignment together. What questions do they suggest?

4. As you begin to ask questions, try to answer them in terms of what you already know. Write out these tentative answers.

5. As you formulate answers, consider other related information that you remember or that comes from assigned readings.

6. Look for the question that most intrigues you. Work with it; write about it. The answer to that question could turn out to be the idea you develop in your essay.

6c Writing and connecting—Combining techniques to find an idea

Ideas most often come to us as we put several techniques together. Questioning, reading, writing, and connecting often go hand in hand.

Joan Didion, a novelist and essayist, says, "I write entirely to find out what I'm thinking." Respecting that exploratory notion of Didion's, consider what can happen when you write with no other purpose at the outset than letting your mind make connections. Let's see how that might look as one student begins to consider a piece of evidence in preparation for developing an idea and writing an essay.

The Writing Assignment–Questioning Photographic Evidence and Making Connections Kristina Wilson had been asked in a second-semester writing class to select an image (a photograph, painting, or sculpture) and bring it to class, described in her own words so that others could see it as she saw it. The exercise was a preliminary step that would lead to an essay about the relationship between an artist and her or his work. To write the essay, Kristina would need an *idea*; to find an idea, she needed *evidence* to consider.

The recreated image—the word-picture brought by the student to class—was to be the *first* piece of evidence that students would investigate. Their task was to look at this initial piece of evidence—the image itself—to question it, and to look again to see what else it might reveal. That questioning was to lead eventually to connections and, finally, to an idea.

Kristina's Response–Questioning to Find an Idea Here is her evidence:

This is an excerpt from Kristina's word picture of Killer Joe Piro—a photograph by Richard Avedon, whose work she had seen during a visit to the Whitney Museum in New York City.

```
     A huge enlargement of Avedon's portrait of the
dancer Killer Joe Piro confronted me, stared at me,
commanded me to really see for once in my life. He
threw his head back and his entire face rushed upward.
His hair became a solid black mass with edges of velvet
grain, and a cowlick of dagger-sharp spikes pointed
downward from the left side of his head. A bit of his
bangs fell forward onto his face, melding and becoming
one with the shadows between the bridge of his nose and
his left eye. Black eyes raced upward as well, reflec-
tions of light in the pupils carving burning paths
in front of him like dividing lines on a highway. He
seemed to have four eyes, six, and at the same time,
none at all. Joe's nose, along with his forehead,
cheeks, and chin, were white hot, scorched into pure
whiteness by intense light. . . . His teeth were play-
ing the same game as his eyes--multiplying and dividing
until they became one and a thousand at the same time.
Those white forms reached upwards and downwards like
stalactites and stalagmites in the dank cave of
Killer's mouth, interspersed with a few needle-thin
```

**Photograph by
Richard Avedon
Killer Joe Piro, dancer
New York City
January 3, 1962
© 1962 Richard Avedon**

```
light smears. His dynamic head rested upon a seemingly
stable half circle of complete darkness, surrounded
by a hint of white collar that disappeared into the
stark white background and the deep black of Killer's
sweater. An ascot ran down an inch or so from his chin,
taking on the look of wood grain as it was smeared,
as if by the hand of some small child, down into the
darkness and off the print.
```

Kristina's vivid description of the photograph ends with this series of interesting questions. Even as she describes her encounter with the photograph, she is already seeing Piro's image as a source of inspiration for her own work as a photographer. She sees motion and light.

```
    I stood in front of him for a long time, trying
to unlock his secrets--how was he moving? How had he
been captured? How could I do work like this? I finally
moved on to view the rest of the exhibit, which
astounded me as well, but I kept finding myself in
front of Joe again, as I do now.
```

In subsequent writing, as she questions the photograph and tries to keep her mind on the essay requirement, which asks her to try to account for Avedon's relationship to the photograph, Kristina worries first about whether she has, in the two years since she first saw the photograph, "seen too much of Killer Joe, if I've exhausted a seemingly inexhaustible resource."

She has a T-shirt with Joe on it and a book about Avedon's photography by Jane Livingston. Killer Joe has "popped up" in her papers and conversations and her thoughts often. The

Livingston book, her own questions about whether too much knowledge interferes with seeing, and a 1995 PBS documentary that she had seen about Avedon's life, lead Kristina, in turn, to more questions about whether Avedon's photographs are not in some way self-portraits, whether all photographs are self-portraits, no matter what the subject.

From the PBS documentary, she recalls Avedon's struggle with "his strong Jewish roots coupled with his lack of native culture or religion and his sense of being the 'loneliest person on earth.'" She concludes tentatively: "So perhaps there is a piece of the photographer in his portrait of Killer Joe—the fleeting moment, the slight look of desperation in Joe's eyes—but I wonder, now that this fact has been revealed to him, how is it that he can continue to photograph so remarkably? How does he, how can *I*, get around knowing too much?"

Looking for a Leading Question or Idea   That last question is the one that intrigues Kristina, and it is the one she tries to answer in her essay. Can photographers avoid being overwhelmed by too much technical and self-knowledge when they go out into the world to take their photographs? Kristina concludes that they can. Her essay develops that conviction.

This review highlights the process that led Kristina to her idea.

- Recall that Kristina began with evidence that she was genuinely interested in. Even though she had looked at that photograph of Piro many times, she chose to look at it again, to see if there was something there she had not seen before.

- She was also looking at the photograph in connection with the requirements of her writing course; that course gave her a line of inquiry, a question to begin with. As she looked and wrote about her questions, she asked more questions.

- She found two other sources of evidence: Jane Livingston's book about Avedon and the PBS documentary. Those sources came into play as she continued to make connections and question the photograph.

- Finally, the questioning led to an idea that she eventually developed in her essay, using as evidence the photograph as well as information from the Livingston book, the documentary, and several other essays that she read in the course.

6d Using collaboration as a way to find ideas

Nothing can spur you on like a friendly but critical collaborator who is willing to give an honest reaction to your writing. That collaborator can save you the misery of self-doubt by pointing out strengths in what you have done. The same person can also help you identify troubling gaps in your writing and offer constructive suggestions for improvement. Most writers thrive on collaborative feedback.

Collaboration is especially effective just before you begin drafting your essay or just after, when you are still trying to develop a good idea. During this searching stage, any one of several collaborators can help you: your instructor, the members of an in-class work group who follow one another's writing (on paper or online), or, if you do not work in groups, one of your classmates.

part

2

Researching: Finding, Evaluating, and Using Sources

7

Understanding Research

Directed research is the formal research you will do to accumulate evidence and develop a thesis on an assigned or selected research topic. Eventually, you will present and defend that thesis—your reasoned conclusion about the accumulated evidence—in a research essay.

Research often begins as you read your required course materials and come upon a topic that intrigues you. Your quest to find out more about this topic can involve such diverse activities as conducting experiments, administering surveys, and undertaking field research; but most often, your search takes you into the library. It may also lead you to the Internet and to the World Wide Web. Once in the library or on the Internet, you can locate books, journals, magazines, newspapers, and other sources that contain additional information on the subject you have chosen or been assigned.

8

Discovering Sources within Your Library

Whether you are starting to do background reading to find a topic, looking for information to help you focus your topic, or preparing to investigate your topic in depth, the library is the place to begin your search.

8a Using the online library catalog

The *library catalog* lists all of a library's holdings, including books, periodicals, cassettes, films, and microforms. All library catalogs list holdings alphabetically three ways: by author, by title, and by subject. Most libraries have transferred the record of their holdings to an online catalog or a microfiche catalog. Follow the on-screen instructions to locate sources.

Many libraries are connected through nationwide computer networks to other libraries' catalogs and to the Online Computer Library Center (OCLC) that links libraries across the country. Smaller, local networks connect affiliated colleges, universities, museums, and institutes that have agreed to pool their research resources. You can request material from other libraries through the ***interlibrary loan service*** provided by your reference librarian.

8b   Using computerized databases

Many libraries now have access to large online database networks. Databases can provide (1) a list of sources related to your topic, (2) abstracts or brief summaries of sources, and (3) the full text of a source that may not be available in your library.

The most widely used database services in academic libraries are the Bibliographic Retrieval Service (BRS) and DIALOG, systems that provide access to hundreds of databases and over a million sources of information. The Research Libraries Information Network (RLIN) also provides a bibliographic database (BIB) and access to many periodicals. Ask a librarian for help with these online database networks.

These services give you immediate access to *Newspaper Abstracts*, *Periodical Abstracts*, the *New York Times Index*, and the *MLA International Bibliography*, among others. For recent additions to online databases and CD-ROM, check *Ulrich's International Periodicals Directory*.

8c   A word of caution

As helpful as database searches can be, they sometimes yield an overwhelming amount of information. Thus, the key words you select for conducting a database search, whether authors, titles, or words related to your subject, should be very specific so that the database does not give you too many sources. Specificity will help make your search manageable. (See 10b for more on key word searches.)

9

Discovering Sources on the Internet and Navigating the Web

The Internet is a vast computer network that can give you access to current events and national news; world news; ongoing research in almost every field; topics of cultural, scientific, and educational interest; library holdings; bibliographies; even conversations among researchers and special-interest groups. This vast network of computers also allows you to send electronic mail (e-mail) to one another.

The Internet connects you to the World Wide Web (abbreviated as WWW, or the Web), a system of linked documents that are placed on the network. These documents, each of which is called a *Web page*, contain information that can supplement and enhance your research, giving you immediate access to library holdings, computer databases, and Web sites. Much of the information on the Web is not in your library.

The first screen you see at a Web site is usually the home page. *Home page* can also refer to the first page you see when you start your *browser*—software, such as Netscape or Internet Explorer, that allows you to search the Internet. The browser uses other software devices, called *search engines*, to go out on the Web and find information. The following are among the most common and most powerful search engines (new engines appear frequently).

AltaVista
http://altavista.com   Very complete and fast search. *Key word and Boolean searching*.

Excite
http://www.excite.com   Easy search of Web pages, reviews, and news groups. *Subject area, key word, and Boolean searching*.

Hotbot
http://hotbot.com   Fast, easy search with many options. E-mail, message boards, chat rooms, home pages. *Subject area, key word, and Boolean searching*.

InfoSeek
http://infoseek.go.com   Searches Web pages, Usenet news groups, FTP and Gopher sites. *Subject area and key word searching. No Boolean searching*.

Lycos
http://lycos.com   One of the largest URL catalogs. *Subject area, key word, and Boolean searching*.

ProFusion
http://profusion.ittc.   Searches multiple engines simultaneously. *Key word and Boolean searching*.
ukans.edu

WebCrawler

http://webcrawler.com   Fast and complete search engine. Includes newsgroups and e-mail. *Subject area, key word, and Boolean searching*.

Yahoo!

http://yahoo.com   Includes news, e-mail, and chat rooms. *Subject area and key word searching. No Boolean searching*.

Today's browsers do most of the searching automatically when you ask for information; they make use of these search engines and other electronic protocols.

As you do your searches, follow the procedures in the accompanying chart. You can modify the search parameters (including the way key words are combined) by following onscreen instructions or the suggestions in 10c. You can also expand your search by selecting a different search engine.

Guidelines for Internet Searches

- Link your computer to the Internet and open your browser.

- From the browser's home page, go to the search box (or follow the browser's procedure for selecting a particular search engine).

- Enter the key words needed for your search (See 10b).

- When the search engine shows a list of its "top" 10 to 25 sites, survey the list to identify the most promising ones. Click on these. The engine may give you more sites (lower in its hierarchy) that are worth pursuing.

- When a site you visit gives you links or references to others that are related, click on the hyperlinks provided (or make a copy of the addresses if there are no direct links).

- After skimming the site you visit, you may decide to print or download its pages for later examination. Note the size and downloading time of the document to be sure it is worthwhile. Also record or store the address and references from the source for later documentation or a return access.

- If you are not satisfied with the first search results, you can (a) try new search words or Boolean combinations (see 10c); (b) try a different search engine on your browser; (c) enter an exact copy of addresses from an earlier search in the browser's address box.

- Do not be afraid to experiment. Retracing your steps on the browser's *back* button or its *home* button may let you pursue another line of inquiry.

10

Narrowing and Refining Your Internet Search

There are three primary ways to facilitate and narrow your searches so that you are only identifying information that is directly related to your research area.

10a Subject area searches

To enhance the earliest phase of library research—as you are trying to find a research topic of interest—you will almost certainly consult the *Library of Congress Subject Headings* (LCSH), a three-volume reference book that lists all of the subject headings used to classify library books. These subject headings provide a good starting point for Internet as well as library searches. The more specific the subject heading, the better.

You can supplement initial library searches by consulting the home pages of most search engines, where you often find a list of organized subject headings that permit you to look quickly for more specific topics that interest you. The home page for Hotbot lists among its many subject areas Art & Entertainment, Business & Money, Health, News & Media, Reference, and Science & Technology. Under each of these subject headings, you will find subtopics. The list of search engines on pages 18–19 identifies additional search engines that support subject-area searches.

10b Key word searches

After you have selected key words that are closely related to your chosen area of research, you are ready for additional searching on the Web. When you enter your key words in the home page window of the search engine, the computer will give you a list of *hits*, each of which serves as a hypertext link to a source of information.

Before searching, consult the home page of the search engine for advance search procedures or for drop-down windows that allow you to customize your search. Also consult the engine's *Help* screen. Unless you restrict searches, you may find more information than you can reasonably consider. A recent search for *gray wolf Yellowstone*, using AltaVista, yielded 2,227,722 Web pages. A more restricted search on the same search engine yielded 472 Web pages. Restricting your topic will help you consolidate your search and expedite your effort to sort and evaluate the information.

10c Boolean searches

Boolean searching allows you to use simple "operators" to restrict your searches. The most common operators are AND, OR, and NOT. These operators work essentially the same way on the Internet as they do when you search the library's online system. However, every search engine has different configurations, requiring that you pay particular attention to minor differences in the way you specify the kind of search you want to conduct and the manner in which you enter the operators.

The underlying principles for Boolean searches remain constant.

- AND (&) limits your search by combining terms: gray AND wolf. This designation ensures that you get sources related only to *gray wolf* (both terms combined). The search would be limited to sources that contain both key words.
- OR (/) expands the search to include any source with either key word: *wolf* OR *Yellowstone*. Both key words would be included in the search.
- NOT (!) limits the search by excluding one term: *wolf* NOT *Yellowstone*. This designation would include all wolves except those associated with Yellowstone.

Always enter Boolean operators in CAPS, with a space between key words and operators. If the designation is highly complex, use parentheses: (*gray* AND *wolf* AND *Yellowstone*) AND (NOT *red* AND *wolf*). Boolean searches can use abbreviations: *wolf* & *Yellowstone*.

Some search engines do not recognize Boolean operators, but permit you to limit searches in other ways. On the home page of the search engine, in a drop-down window, you may find the term *exact phrase*. If you select that option, the search engine will look for the entire key word phrase just as you have entered it into the engine's window: *gray wolf Yellowstone*. If there is no such choice, you may achieve the same effect by placing the key word phrase in quotation marks: "*gray wolf Yellowstone.*" These variations and options will more than likely be explained on the search engine's *Help* screen. If not, experiment.

11
Accessing Your Library's Sources via the Web

Many libraries, both public and academic, make information about their collections available online. However, access to a particular library's holdings is often restricted to library members or to students and members of the faculty.

Often the fastest and most reliable way of obtaining research information is through your own library's Web site. As a student, you will be able to access many of the library's databases as well as many other databases on the Web. The Web page will explain what is available.

One of the simplest ways to determine whether another library's collection is available is to search LibCat, a direct link to information about public, private, and virtual libraries around the world. You can enter over 1,000 academic and public libraries' collections on the Web.

12
Saving Source Information as You Conduct Research

Even during your initial Internet searches, it would be wise to download or copy lists provided by your search engines. The lists are relatively short, contain a great deal of useful information about links, and change often. On your browser, you can also *bookmark* sites as you visit them by clicking *Bookmark* (or *Favorites*), then clicking *Add Bookmark* (or *Add Favorite*). Later, you can find the site quickly by clicking on the bookmark. Having the lists and the bookmarks will save valuable time during subsequent phases of research. Remember also that you will have to document the sources that you use from the Internet; keep track of those sources (see Part 3 for more on documenting sources).

Tips about Downloading and Printing

- Download and store material on your computer to save time and money; you generally pay for the time spent on the Internet.

- Download electronic documents as plain text (rather than storing them with various Internet codes). Your computer should give you choices about the way you want to save the information when you click "Save as" under "Edit."

- Store electronic documents in a designated folder in your computer or on a floppy disk so that you can find them easily. Evaluate the documents later.

- After evaluating the documents, print only the portions that you need for future reference.

- Always keep up with where you found the material on the Internet because you will have to document electronic sources if you use them in your research essay. You may not be able to go back to the Internet at a later date and find the documents. (See 16c and 17b for more on documenting electronic sources.)

13

Evaluating Sources

The accompanying guidelines will help you with your initial assessment of sources.

- Consider the relevance of the source to your restricted topic. Ask yourself whether the source will help you learn more about the topic.

- Consider whether the source is too general or specific for your research needs.

- Check the date of publication. Is the source current? Will current sources serve your purpose, or would older sources be more appropriate? Do you want a combination of older and current sources?

- Look at the author's credentials to establish whether he or she is an authority on the topic. Does the author's name turn up in other sources? If so, that person is probably a reliable expert. You can also check to see what other experts have written about the author.

- Consult a biographical reference book or index for more information on a particular author.
- Ascertain the author's point of view on the topic and whether that point of view seems reasonable. Consider the author's tone and intended audience.
- Do a preliminary source evaluation; scan rather than read the sources in your working bibliography. Scan the table of contents, the preface, the index, the title, notes about the author, subheadings, available abstracts, the afterword, and the listed sources. Once you have eliminated sources that are obviously irrelevant, do a more thorough evaluation of the remaining sources.
- Be sure to record connections you make while scanning or reading. Note these connections and any other ideas about your sources in a reading journal, in a double-column notebook, or on note cards. For any notes that you take, keep track of your sources to avoid unintentional plagiarism.
- Scan electronic sources that you have downloaded and deem reliable (see 13b for more on evaluation of electronic sources). After you judge electronic sources reliable, evaluate their usefulness as you would for any other sources.

13a Reading sources critically

The following tips will help you conduct a more thorough evaluation of your sources that involves reading carefully and critically. (Also see Part 1 on critical reading.)

- Read with an open mind to expand your knowledge of your restricted topic. Be receptive to different points of view and do not take sides—read objectively. Try to distinguish facts from emotional appeals or theories about those facts.
- Question what you are reading. Ask yourself many questions. (See 6b for more on questioning to find an idea.) What is the writer's main idea? How well does the evidence (facts, anecdotes, examples) support the idea?
- Let your reading lead you to other sources. The reference lists at the end of books and articles can alert you to other sources.
- Write as you read. Take notes that can be incorporated into your essay. These notes can also include your comments and reflections about that evidence.
- Think about the relevance and reliability of your sources using the evaluation guidelines. Continue to weed out unusable sources.

A good rule of thumb to apply when you are evaluating documents (in your library and on the World Wide Web) has to do with *reliability*. A source can be considered reliable when you and your audience are sufficiently convinced of its truth or value to act on it. Because we know that truth or value can be relative (different people looking at the same piece of information may see its value quite differently), you must be very careful to consider viewpoints other than your own when judging a document's reliability. Check what you read against other information that you find in your research; check it, too, against the demands of special-interest groups who have a vested interest in your topic but may not agree with your point of view.

13b Special precautions about electronic sources

The biggest problem you face as you confront this vast array of information on the Web is how to evaluate it, how to judge its reliability. Be especially wary of anonymous documents; remember that anyone can post information on the Internet. Because the information is often new and has not been processed and subjected to the scrutiny of rigorous review, you must be careful about using it uncritically; it is often not as reliable as the information you find in printed sources in the library, which have often been subject to review processes, including judgment by other scholars.

14

Taking Notes

As you critically read sources and determine their usefulness, you will want to take notes. Thorough and accurate note-taking during research will help you once you start writing the research essay and when you need to acknowledge your sources.

As you take notes, always try to distill your sources into a form you can use later in your essay, such as a *summary*, a *paraphrase*, a *direct quotation*, or *reflections* on what you are reading— or a combination of these (see Part 1 for more on critical reading).

Always record your notes carefully and accurately so that you will not have to waste valuable time later going back to the original sources to clarify confusing entries or to fill in gaps.

Accurate notes will help you avoid accidental *plagiarism*—
borrowing from a source without giving proper credit.

Note-taking is not a mechanical process of copying from
your sources to your note cards. You should be doing a great
deal of thinking and reflecting as you read and take notes. As
you read and think about your sources, try to make connections
between ideas. Develop a system of cross-referencing that will
permit you to keep track of the connections you make as you
proceed with your research.

15

Incorporating Sources

The process of incorporating evidence always requires
that you pare down the source—by selecting a passage, a phrase,
or just a word that you will quote, or by distilling the essence
of the source in the form of a summary or a paraphrase. Often,
writers use a combination of these techniques.

15a Summarizing

When you *summarize* a source, you condense a fairly
lengthy passage of text into a few sentences of your own words.
A summary is always shorter than the original source; it strives
to capture the essence of the source. Follow these guidelines
for summarizing.

- Read the source, looking for the writer's main idea.
- As you read, note key words, striking images, and impor-
  tant sentences.
- In your own words, write down the main idea of the passage.
- Test your summary of the main idea during a second reading. Carefully check the summary against the passage itself.
  Make sure you have captured the essence of the passage.
- A summary is a substantially shortened version of the
  source but includes sufficient information so that your
  reader can understand the source.
- If you decide to incorporate a few of the writer's key words
  or phrases into your summary, be sure to enclose them in
  quotation marks and record the page numbers in parentheses right after the closing quotation marks.
- Be sure you have an entry in your working bibliography for
  the source.

15b Paraphrasing

A *paraphrase* does the same thing as a summary but follows the structure of the original source—the particular order the writer uses to reach a conclusion, develop an idea, or create emphasis. As you paraphrase, follow the accompanying guidelines.

- Read the source, looking for the writer's main idea.
- Write down, in your own words and using your own sentence structure, what you think the main idea is. Order your paraphrase just as the original source is ordered; include appropriate details.
- Check your paraphrase against the source. Make sure that you have captured the essence of the source and that your wording differs significantly from the wording in the original source.
- Include sufficient information in your paraphrase so that your reader can understand the source.
- Avoid plagiarism by giving credit to the author of the paraphrased material. Note source page numbers. If you include important terms and phrases from the source, put those words in quotation marks.
- Reflect on the source, but be sure to separate your reflections and paraphrase.
- Be sure you have an entry in your working bibliography for the source.

15c Quoting

When you *quote*, record a writer's exact words, being careful to preserve the punctuation marks, capitalization, and spelling in the original. Enclose the writer's words in quotation marks. The length of a quotation can vary from a single word to several paragraphs.

Several reasons to quote rather than summarize or paraphrase are outlined in the following list. Use quotations sparingly. However, you should quote when:

- The writer's words are so cogent and memorable that summarizing or paraphrasing would undercut their effectiveness or alter their meaning.
- You believe the writer's words will lend authority to what you have to say and will be more persuasive than your summary or paraphrase of those words.
- You want to take exception to what a writer has said.

- You want to comment on a writer's words as a way of expressing your own position or idea.
- You want to let a speaker's own words expose the weakness of his or her argument.
- You want to cite statistical information from the source.

15d Reflecting

Reflecting on your sources is an important part of the process of taking useful notes. When you reflect, you enter into a conversation with the source you are reading; you think carefully about the source, trying to make connections with other sources, to relate ideas that come to mind, to clarify and gain insight. Learn to listen to these thoughts. In doing so you become an active, critical reader who hears a text and your mind's reaction to it. (See Part 1 for more on reading.)

Noting your reflections on sources will prove beneficial when the time comes to organize and write your research essay. From these reflections, you can find ideas and discover patterns and additional connections. Your research essay will not merely be a compilation of the ideas of other writers and researchers; it will contain what *you* think about your sources. Maintaining a record of your reflections as you take notes will help you make sense of your research; it will help you make the leap from the ideas and words of others to your own ideas.

When you record your reflections in your notes, be sure always to distinguish them from the information you take directly from the sources in the form of summaries, paraphrases, or quotations. Always take care to avoid plagiarism.

16
MLA Documentation Style

The method of documentation described and illustrated in this section is recommended by the Modern Language Association in its *MLA Handbook for Writers of Research Papers* (5th ed. New York: MLA, 1999). MLA documentation style is used both in student papers and in scholarly articles in literature and languages. Consult the accompanying chart that lists MLA forms for an overview of the types of citations described in this section.

Directory of MLA In-text, Parenthetical Citations

16a MLA style for in-text, parenthetical citations

MLA style uses two methods for citing borrowed material within the text: (1) The author and page number of the source are identified immediately following the borrowed material. (2) The author is identified in the text and the page reference is given immediately following the borrowed material. In-text citations guide readers to the appropriate source in the Works Cited list where readers can get the bibliographic information they need to locate the material within a particular source.

Use the following guidelines when writing with parenthetical citations.

- Keep the citations concise, but provide all necessary information.
- Use an author's last name in the first and subsequent in-text citations. Use an author's first initial and last name if two authors in the Works Cited list share the same last name.
- Punctuate and format the parenthetical citations in the following manner.
    1. Place the parenthetical citation either at the end of the sentence or at a natural pause within the sentence. In either case, the citation should follow, as closely as possible, the material it refers to.
    2. When the citation is placed immediately following a quotation, place the citation after the closing quotation marks.
    3. Place any punctuation marks in the text immediately following the closing parenthesis of the citation.
    4. In block quotations, place the parenthetical citation after the final punctuation mark of the quotation.
    5. Include a page reference for the borrowed material.

1. Author not named in text

When the author is not named in the text, place that author's last name and the page reference in parentheses, at a point where the citation does not interrupt the flow of your writing. Do not use a comma or the abbreviations *p.* or *pp.* within the parentheses.

```
Hawthorne's son Julian recalled that his father read
novels for relaxation, but that he seriously studied
popular newspapers and magazines (Reynolds 114).
```

2. Author named in text

If the author is identified in the text, cite only the page number in parentheses.

```
Herzog notes that there are more protests against
experiments on domestic animals like dogs and cats
than against research involving animals like
snakes (349).
```

3. Entire work

When citing an entire work such as a complete article or book rather than a particular passage within the work, do not refer to the work within a parenthetical citation. The source must be cited in the Works Cited list.

Bennett and Ames survey the use and abuse of alcohol in various cultures.

4. Work with two or three authors

Include the last name of each author in the text or in a citation.

Lichtenstein and Danker have noted that beginning in 1974, the New Orleans Center for the Creative Arts (NOCCA) has produced successful performers such as Wynton Marsalis and Harry Connick, Jr. (284).

Classroom research can be done most effectively when one becomes a "participant observer" (Cohn, Kottkamp, and Provenzo 89-91).

5. Work with four or more authors

When citing a work with four or more authors, either list the last name of each author or list the author whose name appears first on the title page, followed by *et al.* (meaning "and others").

A pregnant adolescent "experiences restricted social relationships and less positive interactions with both friends and family" and so is subject to severe emotional stress (Passino et al. 118).

6. Multivolume work

Cite the author, volume number, and page reference (Hamilton 26: 293). Separate the volume number and the page reference by a colon followed by one space. Do not use the words *volume* or *pages* or the abbreviations *vol.* or *p.* when referring to passages within a volume. An arabic number to the left of the colon identifies the volume and a number to the right of the colon indicates the page number(s).

Alexander Hamilton may have foreseen the fatal result of his duel with Aaron Burr because on 4 July 1804 he wrote to his wife: "Fly to the bosom of your God and be comforted" (26: 293).

To refer to an entire volume of a multivolume work, follow the author's name with a comma and the abbreviation *vol.* (Hamilton, vol. 3). Do not abbreviate *volume* when using the word in text: "In volume 3, Hamilton mentions [. . .] ."

7. Anonymous work

Cite an anonymous work by its title, which may be shortened to a key defining word or phrase (as is the article "Democracy and Mega-Scandal" in the following example).

```
The truth about the Contras, Iran, Star Wars, and other
controversies will probably never be known ("Democracy" 6-8).
```

8. Corporate author

It is best to cite the name of a corporate, or collective, author in the text rather than in a long parenthetical reference.

```
A 1990 report by the State Board of Education of New
York urges curricular revisions that emphasize multi-
culturalism (2-4).
```

9. Indirect citation

When quoting from an indirect or secondary source (such as an author's report of someone else's statement), use the abbreviation *qtd. in* (meaning "quoted in") and then cite the source. Always identify the original writer or speaker in the text or citation.

```
Robert Coughlan wrote that Faulkner "acts like a farmer
who had studied Plato and looks like a river gambler"
(qtd. in Blotner 2: 1468).
```

10. Literary work

Give the page number(s) from the edition of the work that is being cited. Because some literary works exist in many different editions, it is helpful to follow the page numbers with a semicolon and appropriate abbreviations for major divisions of the work (210; ch. 15) or (5; act 1). For a poem, cite line number(s) and in your first reference use the word *line(s)*.

For verse plays, do not use page numbers. Give the act, scene, and line numbers separated by periods.

```
Hamlet's last words are "the rest is silence" (5.2.247).
```

11. Author of two or more cited works

To distinguish among multiple works by an author, include the title or a shortened title in an in-text phrase or in a parenthetical citation.

```
Kingston describes how she had to learn the appropriate
cultural behavior for a Chinese-American female (Woman
35-40).
```

In this example, *Woman* is an abbreviated form of Maxine Hong Kingston's book entitled *The Woman Warrior.*

12. Authors with the same last name

When two or more authors cited in a paper have the same last name, include the author's first name in a brief in-text phrase or in a parenthetical citation. To distinguish Larry L.

King from Martin Luther King, Jr., for example, do the following.

```
In his essay "American Redneck," Larry L. King describes
his early manhood.
```

Do the same for parenthetical citations.

```
"American Redneck" (L. King) describes a young writer's
experiences.
```

13. Two or more sources in a single citation

In referring to more than one source in parentheses, include information for both sources, separated by semicolons.

```
Recent interpretations of Shakespeare's The Tempest
consider the play's racist implications (Takaki 52;
Greenblatt 121).
```

14. Nonprint source

Provide enough information for readers to locate the source in the Works Cited list.

```
The TV series The Civil War includes a moving letter
written by Sullivan Ballou to his wife shortly before
his death.
```

16b MLA style for explanatory and reference notes

Explanatory Notes

Explanatory notes are used for comments or information that would be disruptive if placed in the body of the paper. Explanatory notes can be used to clarify, illustrate, or further explain an idea; to provide definitions; or to identify individuals and events. Avoid overusing explanatory notes because they can distract from the main text of the essay.

Use a superscript arabic number immediately after the term or passage to be expanded upon. That number corresponds to a list of notes placed at the end of the paper (endnotes). Head this separate page "Notes" and place it immediately before the Works Cited list. (The corresponding list of notes could be placed at the bottom of the typewritten page and called footnotes.)

TEXT WITH SUPERSCRIPT

```
The Volstead Act provided for enforcement of the
Eighteenth Amendment by empowering federal agents to
prosecute bootleggers and other violators.[1]
```

EXPLANATORY NOTE
[1]The law, passed in 1919, was named for its sponsor, Andrew Joseph Volstead, congressman from Minnesota.

Reference Notes

Reference notes direct readers to additional sources and often to another section of an essay. References that support an essay's ideas usually include the word *see*, and those that contradict an essay's ideas include the word *compare*. A source named in a reference note should be included in the Works Cited list. These notes are formatted like explanatory notes.

TEXT WITH SUPERSCRIPT
Mark Twain was convinced that the novels of Sir Walter Scott had infected the South with false romantic notions.[2]

REFERENCE NOTE: BOOK
[2]For a full account of Twain's opinion of Scott, see Krause 145-49.

Directory of MLA Works Cited Sample Entries

(continued)

16c   MLA style for the Works Cited list

All the sources cited in a paper should be listed at the end of the paper. This separate listing is called the "Works Cited" list. A concluding list of sources that were examined but not cited in a paper is called a "Works Consulted" list. In a typical research paper a single listing of Works Cited is all that is required.

Following the last page of the paper and any concluding notes, begin the list with the title "Works Cited" without quotation marks or underlining, centered, and an inch from the top of the page. The Works Cited list is paginated as the rest of the paper. Double-space between the title and the first entry.

Arrange the citation entries in alphabetical order by authors' last names. If a source is anonymous, alphabetize it by the first major word in its title (not *a*, *an*, or *the*). Begin each entry flush with the left margin, but indent all subsequent lines of the entry one-half inch (or five typed spaces). Double-space between entries. Sample Works Cited entries for books, periodicals, and other sources follow.

Books

A standard MLA entry for a book consists of three elements: author, title, and publication information. These three elements are separated from one another by a period and one space. The entry concludes with a period.

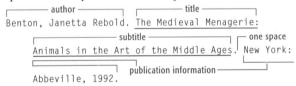

```
┌────── author ──────┐   ┌────── title ──────┐
Benton, Janetta Rebold. The Medieval Menagerie:

┌────────── subtitle ──────────┐  ┌ one space
Animals in the Art of the Middle Ages. New York:

┌──────────────────┐ publication information ─┘
    Abbeville, 1992.
```

Keep the following guidelines in mind when preparing book entries for the Works Cited list.

1. **Author:** An author's name (exactly as it appears on the title page) should appear last name first, followed by a comma, then by the first and middle names or initials. Put a period after the author's name.

2. **Title:** Copy the title and subtitle (if any) from the title page, not from the cover or spine of the book. Underline the title and capitalize all major words. Separate the main title from the subtitle with a colon. Put a period after the title and subtitle.

3. **Publication information:** Copy the publication information (the city of publication, the publisher, and the year of publication) from the title and copyright pages. If more than one city is listed on the title page, cite the first one only. Put a colon and one space after the city of publication before the publisher's name. Abbreviate or shorten names of publishers by dropping articles and words such as *Press* and abbreviations

such as *Co.* ("Bantam Books, Inc." becomes "Bantam"), using only the last names of persons ("Charles Scribner's Sons" becomes "Scribner's"), and by using only the first in a string of last names ("Harcourt Brace Jovanovich, Inc." becomes "Harcourt"). Abbreviate "University Press" so that it reads "UP." If the publisher is an imprint of another publisher (as Belknap Press is an imprint of Harvard University Press), include both publisher names separated by a hyphen ("Belknap-Harvard UP") in the Works Cited list. The publisher's name is followed by a comma, one space, and the most recent year of publication.

1. Book with one author

Benton, Janetta Rebold. The Medieval Menagerie: Animals
    in the Art of the Middle Ages. New York:
    Abbeville, 1992.

2. Book with two or three authors

Lichtenstein, Grace, and Laura Danker. Musical Gumbo:
    The Music of New Orleans. New York: Norton, 1993.

McCrum, William, William Cran, and Robert MacNeil.
    The Story of English. New York: Viking, 1986.

3. Book with more than three authors

Bendure, Glenda, et al. Scandinavian and Baltic Europe
    on a Shoestring. Berkeley: Lonely Planet, 1993.

4. Book with an anonymous author

The World Almanac and Book of Facts. New York: NEA,
    1983.

5. Book with an author and an editor

Orwell, George. Orwell: The War Commentaries. Ed. W. J.
    West. New York: Pantheon, 1985.

If the in-text citations generally refer to the editor instead of the author, begin the entry with the editor's name.

West, W. J., ed. Orwell: The War Commentaries. By
    George Orwell. New York: Pantheon, 1985.

6. Book with an editor

Bennett, Linda A., and Genevieve M. Ames, eds. The
    American Experience with Alcohol: Contrasting
    Cultural Perspectives. New York: Plenum, 1985.

7. Selection from an anthology

Chrisman, Noel J. "Alcoholism: Illness or Disease?"
    The American Experience with Alcohol: Contrasting
    Cultural Perspectives. Ed. Linda A. Bennett and
    Genevieve M. Ames. New York: Plenum, 1985. 7-21.

8. Two or more selections from an anthology

Bennett, Linda A., and Genevieve M. Ames, eds. <u>The
      American Experience with Alcohol: Contrasting
      Cultural Perspectives</u>. New York: Plenum, 1985.

Freund, Paul J. "Polish-American Drinking: Continuity
      and Change." Bennett and Ames 77-92.

Stivers, Richard. "Historical Meanings of Irish-American
      Drinking." Bennett and Ames 109-29.

9. Book with a corporate author

National Geographic Society. <u>Discovering Britain and
      Ireland</u>. Washington: Natl. Geog. Soc., 1985.

10. Book in a series

Gannon, Susan R., and Ruth Anne Thompson. <u>Mary Mapes
      Dodge</u>. Twayne's United States Authors Ser. 604.
      New York: Twayne-Macmillan, 1993.

11. Book with a title within the title

Renza, Louis A. <u>"A White Heron" and the Question of
      Minor Literature</u>. Madison: U of Wisconsin P, 1984.

McCarthy, Patrick A., ed. <u>Critical Essays on James Joyce's</u>
      Finnegan's Wake. New York: Hall, 1992.

12. Two or more books by the same author

Woodward, C. Vann. <u>The Future of the Past</u>. New York:
      Oxford UP, 1989.

---. <u>Origins of the New South</u>. 1951. Baton Rouge:
      Louisiana State UP, 1971.

---. <u>Reunion and Reaction</u>. Boston: Little, 1966.

13. Multivolume book

Malone, Dumas. <u>Jefferson and His Time</u>. 6 vols. Boston:
      Little, 1943-77.

14. Translation

Wilhelm, Richard. <u>Confucius and Confucianism</u>. Trans.
      George H. Danton and Annina Periam Danton. New
      York: Harcourt, 1931.

15. Revised edition

Holloway, Mark. <u>Heavens on Earth: Utopian Communities
      in America, 1660-1880</u>. 2nd ed. New York:
      Dover, 1966.

16. Republished book

Austen, Jane. <u>Emma</u>. 1816. New York: Penguin, 1986.

17. Preface, foreword, introduction, or afterword

Monette, Paul. Foreword. <u>A Rock and a Hard Place: One
    Boy's Triumphant Story</u>. By Anthony Godby Johnson.
    New York: Crown-Random, 1993. xiii-xvii.

18. Article in a reference book

"Cochise." <u>Encyclopedia of Indians of the Americas</u>.
    St. Clair Shores, MI: Scholarly, 1974.

19. Government publication

United States. Dept. of Commerce. <u>U.S. Industrial Out-
    look '92: Business Forecasts for 350 Industries</u>.
    Washington: GPO, 1992.

United States. Cong. House. Committee on Ways and Means.
    <u>Hearings on Comprehensive Tax Reform</u>. 106th Cong.,
    1st sess. 9 vols. Washington: GPO, 1986.

Periodicals

Periodicals such as scholarly journals, magazines, and
newspapers supply useful, up-to-date information for research
essays. Like the listing for a book, a basic Works Cited entry
for a periodical consists of three elements: author, title, and publication information. These three elements are separated from
one another by a period. The entry ends with a period.

```
┌───── author ──────┐  ┌──────────── title ────────────┐
Panikkar, Raimundo. "There Is No Outer without
indent 5 ──────────────┐  ┌───── publication information ─────┐
spaces
 |   Inner Space." Cross Currents 43 (1993): 60-81.
```

Keep the following guidelines in mind when preparing periodical entries for the Works Cited list.

1. **Author:** An author's name should appear last name first, followed by a comma, then by the first and middle names or initials. Put a period after the author's name.

2. **Title:** Enclose the article title (and subtitle, if any) within
   quotation marks, and capitalize all major words. Put a period
   at the end of the title, inside the closing quotation mark, followed by the publication information.

3. **Publication information:** Include the periodical title (copied
   from its cover), underlined, with introductory articles deleted
   (*New York Times,* not *The New York Times*); follow with one
   space. If appropriate, give the volume and issue numbers, followed by one space. Give the year of publication, in parentheses, followed by a colon and one space. For magazines and
   newspapers, list the day and month (abbreviated except for
   May, June, and July) of publication, with the day before the
   month, the month before the year (19 Dec. 1999). End the

entry with inclusive page numbers of the entire article; do not use the abbreviations *p.* or *pp.*

20. *Article in a journal paginated by volume*

Williams, Adelia. "Jean Tardieu: The Painterly Poem."
    Foreign Language Studies 18 (1991): 114-25.

21. *Article in a journal paginated by issue*

Bender, Daniel. "Diversity Revisited, or Composition's
    Alien History." Rhetoric Review 12.1 (1987):
    108-24.

22. *Article in a magazine*

Howard, Bill. "Portable Computing: Power without the
    Pounds." PC Magazine Aug. 1993: 125-269.

Use the symbol "+" to indicate discontinuous paging when an article is interrupted and continues later in the magazine.

Jennings, Andrew. "Old Money and Murder in Chechnia."
    Nation 20 Sept. 1993: 265+.

23. *Article with multiple authors*

Passino, Anne Wurtz, et al. "Personal Adjustment during
    Pregnancy and Adolescent Parenting." Adolescence
    28 (1993): 97-122.

24. *Article with a title within the title*

Hicks, David. "'Seeker for He Knows Not What': Hawthorne's
    Criticism of Emerson in the Summer of 1842."
    Nathaniel Hawthorne Review 17.1 (1991): 1-4.

25. *Article in a newspaper*

Claiborne, William. "Boxes Full of Conspiracy?
    Researchers Dig into JFK Assassination Papers."
    Washington Post 24 Aug. 1993: A1+.

26. *Article with an anonymous author*

"Democracy and Mega-Scandal." New Yorker 27 Sept. 1993:
    6-8.

"Nissan Motors May Sell Some Stockholdings." Wall Street
    Journal 10 Sept. 1993: B4.

27. *Editorial*

"Another Tug-of-War over a Child." Editorial. Chicago
    Tribune 7 Sept. 1993: 20.

28. *Letter to the editor*

Weber, Carl. "In Health Care, U.S. Is Best." Letter.
    New York Times 30 May 1990: A25.

29. Review

Jefferson, Margo. "The Department Store and the Culture
    It Created." Rev. of Land of Desire: Merchants,
    Power and the Rise of a New American Culture, by
    William Leach. New York Times 1 Dec. 1993: C24.

Rothstein, Edward. "Blood and Thunder from the Young
    Verdi." Rev. of I Lombardi. Metropolitan Opera
    House, New York. New York Times 4 Dec. 1993: C11.

Other Sources

30. Interview

Salter, James. "James Salter: The Art of Fiction XCCCIII."
    Interview. Paris Review 127 (1993): 54-100.

Selzer, Richard. Telephone interview. 7 Jan. 1992.

31. A published letter

Keats, John. "To Benjamin Bailey." 22 Nov. 1817. Letter
    31 of The Letters of John Keats. Ed. Maurice Buxton
    Forman. 4th ed. London: Oxford UP, 1952. 66-69.

32. A personal letter

Dillard, Annie. Letter to the author. 10 Apr. 1988.

33. Lecture or speech

Anstendig, Linda. "Curriculum Design for the '90s:
    Developing Personal Growth and Social Conscious-
    ness." Conf. on College Composition and
    Communication. Boston. 19 Mar. 1991.

34. Unpublished dissertation

Martin, Rebecca E. "The Spectacle of Suffering: Repeti-
    tion and Closure in the Eighteenth-Century Gothic
    Novel." Diss. CUNY, 1994.

35. Published dissertation

Kauta, John B. Analysis and Assessment of the Concept
    of Revelation in Karl Rahner's Theology: Its
    Application and Relationship to African Tradi-
    tional Religions. Diss. Fordham U, 1992. Ann
    Arbor: UMI, 1993. 9300240.

36. Dissertation abstract

Jenkins, Douglas Joseph. "Soldier Theatricals: 1940-1945."
    Diss. Bowling Green State U. DAI 53 (1993): 4133A.

37. Performance

In the Summer House. By Jane Bowles. Dir. JoAnne Akalaitis.
    Perf. Dianne Wiest, Alina Arenal, and Jaime Tirelli.
    Vivian Beaumont Theatre, New York. 1 Aug. 1993.

Slatkin, Leonard, cond. St. Louis Symphony Orchestra.
    Concert. Carnegie Hall, New York. 23 Oct. 1994.

38. Musical composition

Beethoven, Ludwig van. Symphony no. 5 in C minor, op. 67.

Mozart, Wolfgang Amadeus. Don Giovanni.

39. Work of art

Bernini, Gianlorenzo. Apollo and Daphne. Galleria
    Borghese, Rome.

Moses, Grandma. The Barn Dance. Hammer Galleries, New
    York. Grandma Moses. By Otto Kallir. New York:
    Abrams, 1973. Illustration 940.

40. Film

The Age of Innocence. Dir. Martin Scorsese. Prod.
    Barbara DeFina. Perf. Daniel Day-Lewis, Michelle
    Pfeiffer, and Winona Ryder. Columbia, 1993.

Scorsese, Martin, dir. The Age of Innocence. Prod.
    Barbara DeFina. Perf. Daniel Day-Lewis, Michelle
    Pfeiffer, and Winona Ryder. Columbia, 1993.

41. Television or radio program

48 Hours: State of Fear. Narr. Dan Rather. CBS. WHDH,
    Boston. 8 Dec. 1993.

Chantilly Lace. Dir. Linda Yellen. Prod. Steven Hewitt.
    Perf. Lindsay Crouse, Jill Eikenberry, and Martha
    Plimpton. Showtime. New York. 18 July 1993.

Friedson, Michael, and Felice Friedson. Jewish Horizons.
    WWNN-AM, Fort Lauderdale. 19 Sept. 1993.

42. Recording

Bartoli, Cecilia. The Impatient Lover: Italian Songs by
    Beethoven, Schubert, Haydn, and Mozart. Compact
    disc. London, 440 297-2, 1993.

Gaines, Ernest. A Gathering of Old Men. American Audio
    Prose Library, 6051, 1986.

43. Videotape or videocassette

The Dakota Conflict. Narr. Garrison Keillor. Video-
    cassette. Filmic Archives, 1992.

44. Map or chart

France. Map. Chicago: Rand, 1988.

45. Cartoon

Trudeau, Garry. "Doonesbury." Cartoon. Boston Globe
    19 Sept. 1994: 23.

Electronic Sources

The MLA "Works Cited" system (as described in the *MLA Handbook for Writers of Research Papers*, *5th ed.*) distinguishes electronic citation forms according to whether the material is available on a CD-ROM or diskette or whether it is available through various channels online.

Because electronic media are continually changing, the details of citations may evolve even as the basic needs for citing references stay the same. Whatever the medium, researchers using electronic material need to provide complete data to identify a source and give clear and consistent directions for locating it wherever it has been found. With this in mind, it is important to include two dates in these citations: the date of electronic publication (or of its latest update) and the date of access to that publication.

Electronic sources require the same critical scrutiny as do print sources, but evaluation of the reliability of electronic sources is sometimes more difficult. See Chapter 13 for guidance on evaluating electronic sources.

> 46. *CD-ROM, tape, or diskette produced as a one-time publication*

Mann, Ron. <u>Poetry in Motion II</u>. CD-ROM. New York:
    Voyager. 1995.

> 47. *CD-ROM, tape, or diskette updated periodically, which also has a print equivalent*

Lacayo, Richard. "This Land Is Whose Land?" <u>Time</u>
    23 Oct. 1995: 68-71. <u>Academic ASAP</u>. CD-ROM.
    Infotrac. Dec. 1995.

> 48. *CD-ROM, tape, or diskette updated periodically, which has no print equivalent*

Levi Strauss. "The Levi Strauss Co.: Balance Sheet,
    1/1/95-12/31/95." <u>Compact Disclosure</u>. CD-ROM. New
    York: Digital Library Systems. Jan. 1996.

When you cite a multi-disk publication, include the total number of disks or the disk number if you use only one.

<u>Perseus 2.0: Interactive Sources and Studies on
    Ancient Greece</u>. CD-ROM. 4 disks. New Haven: Yale
    UP, 1996.

> 49. *Online sources*

ONLINE SCHOLARLY PROJECT OR REFERENCE DATABASE
<u>Britannica Online</u>. Vers. 97.1.1. Mar. 1997. Encyclope-
    dia Britannica. 3 June 1998 <http://www.eb.com/>.

Internet Classics Archive. Ed. Daniel C. Stevenson.
  3 July 1998. MIT Program in Writing and Humanistic
  Studies, Massachusetts Institute of Technology.
  29 Oct. 1999 <http://classics.mit.edu/index.html>.

ONLINE PROFESSIONAL OR PERSONAL SITE

Chang, Kyle A. Home page. 4 June 1998
  <http://www.stern.nyu.edu/~kac227/>.

A Guide to Contemporary Art in New England. 5 June 1998
  <http://nearts.com>.

NYU Web. New York University. 3 June 1998
  <http://www.nyu.edu/>.

ONLINE BOOK

Fielding, Henry. The History of Tom Jones, a Foundling.
  1749. 29 Oct. 1999 <http://www.vt.edu/vt98/
  academics/books/fielding/tom_jones>.

To cite a book that is part of a scholarly project, follow the
style for online books, but include information about the project after the publication information about the book and before the book's URL or Internet address.

Sophocles. Antigone. Trans. R. C. Jebb. Internet
  Classics Archive. MIT Program in Writing
  and Humanistic Studies. 29 Oct. 1999 <http://
  classics.mit.edu/Sophocles/antigone.html>.

ARTICLE IN AN ONLINE PERIODICAL

In general, follow the procedure for citing print periodicals and modify them by adding date of access and the electronic
address.

ARTICLE IN A SCHOLARLY JOURNAL

Barnard, Rita. "Another Country: Amnesia and Memory
  in Contemporary South Africa." Postmodern Culture
  9.1 (1998). 29 Oct. 1999 <http://etexta.ohiolink.
  edu:6873/journals/postmodern_culture/v009/
  9.1r_barnard.html>.

NEWSGROUP/USENET POSTING

Bloom, Eric. "Unreal Computer Game." Online
  posting. 30 May 1998. 7 June 1998
  <news:comp.edu.languages.natural>.

LISTSERV DISCUSSION MESSAGE

McCarty, Willard. "One More Than Ten." Online posting.
  7 May 1998. Humanist Discussion Group. 7 June 1998
  <http://lists. village.virginia.edu/lists_archive/
  Humanist/v12/2000.html>.

PERSONAL E-MAIL

Hoy, Pat. "Re: Mentoring." E-mail to Marion Bishop. 31
  May 1998.

SYNCHRONOUS COMMUNICATION (MOOS, MUDS, IRC)

Haynes-Burton, Cynthia (Cyn). Online conference on
    text-based reality "Writing and Community: The Use
    of MOOs in the Teaching of Writing." 30 Apr. 1995.
    LinguaMOO. 8 June 1998 <http://wwwpub.utdallas.edu/
    ~cynthiah/lingua_archive/Meridian-moo-seminar.txt>.

16d MLA manuscript format

SAMPLE FIRST PAGE IN MLA STYLE

1 inch

½ inch

Kostka 1

Ericka Kostka
Professor Ed Miller
Expos 16, Section 10
December 20, 1997

◄—1 inch—►

Double-space

> Preserving the Wild:
> The Gray Wolf in Yellowstone

indent
5 spaces
or one-
half inch

The vapors that drift visibly from
Yellowstone's Mammoth Hot Springs re-   ◄—1 inch—►
mind me to take shallow breaths so as
not to burn my lungs with sulfur-choked
air. My eyes at times can only barely
adjust to the glare of the sun on Hell-
roaring Creek. Adjustments are invari-
ably in order when people and nature
come into contact. My purpose for ven-
turing to Yellowstone was to experience
its wild beauty, so I adapted myself to
it. But when we hold our own intentions
primary, the concessions can tilt
harshly the other way.

> The elimination of the gray wolf
from Yellowstone National Park during
the early part of this century marked
a major ecological concession to the
interests of stockgrowers. Wolves wandered freely throughout Yellowstone for
two million years until the government
launched an intensive extermination effort. Because of their predatory nature,
wolves were regarded as "a decided men-
ace to the herds of elk, deer, moun-
tain sheep, and antelope" (McNamee 12).
Government hunters used guns, traps,
and poisons during their war on Yellowstone wolves between 1915 and 1926.

SAMPLE MLA WORKS CITED LIST

MLA-style Works Cited
appears on a separate page;
heading is centered

Works Cited

Bader, Harry R. "Wolf Conservation: The
    Importance of Following Endangered
    Species Recovery Plans." <u>Harvard
    Environmental Law Review</u> 13 (1989):
    517-33.

Cauble, Christopher. "Return of the Native."
    <u>National Parks</u> July-Aug. 1986: 24-29.

Edwards, Diane. "Recall of the Wild Wolf."
    <u>Science News</u> 13 June 1987: 378-79.

Gallagher, Winifred. "Return of the Wild."
    <u>Mother Earth</u> Sept./Oct. 1990: 34+.

Lopez, Barry. <u>Of Wolves and Men</u>. New York:
    Scribner's, 1978.

McIntyre, Rick. <u>A Society of Wolves:
    National Parks and the Battle over
    the Wolf</u>. Stillwater: Voyageur, 1993.

McNamee, Thomas. <u>The Return of the Wolf to
    Yellowstone</u>. New York: Holt, 1997.

---. "Yellowstone's Missing Element."
    <u>Audubon</u> Jan. 1986: 12+.

Mech, L. David. Foreword. <u>Wolves</u>. By Can-
    dace Savage. San Francisco: Sierra
    Club, 1988.

Parnall, Peter. "A Wolf in the Eye."
    <u>Audubon</u> Jan. 1988: 78+.

Satchell, Michael. "The New Call of the
    Wild." <u>U.S. News & World Report</u> 29
    Oct. 1990: 29.

Schlickeisen, Rodger. "Wolf Recovery's
    Significance." <u>Defenders Magazine</u>
    Summer 1997. 9 Oct. 1997 <http://www.
    defenders.org/defenders/rssu97.html>.

Schneider, Bill. "The Return of the Wolf."
    <u>National Parks</u> July/Aug. 1981: 7+.

U.S. Fish and Wildlife Service. "Gray Wolf
    Recovery: Weekly Progress Report.
    Week October 28-November 3, 1997."
    <u>IWC Yellowstone Updates</u> 17 Nov. 1997.
    <http://www.wolf.org/wolfnews/
    ystone/ylwoct28.html>.

Williams, Ted. "Waiting for Wolves to Howl
    in Yellowstone." <u>Audubon</u> Nov. 1990: 32+.

Entries in
alphabetical
order, by
authors' names

Last names,
first; followed
by comma and
first name

First line of each
entry is flush
with left margin

Subsequent
lines of each
entry are
indented five
spaces

17

APA Documentation Style

The documentation style described in this section is that recommended in the *Publication Manual of the American Psychological Association* (4th ed. Washington: APA, 1994). This system, usually referred to as APA style, is used in psychology and in other social science disciplines, such as anthropology and sociology. But because variations exist among the documentation styles in the social sciences, you should check with your instructor about his or her preferred documentation style before beginning your paper.

Like the MLA style, the APA style includes brief in-text, parenthetical citations of borrowed material and lists at the end of the paper the sources cited. APA style, however, uses fewer abbreviations than does the MLA style. In addition, some publication data are included in APA parenthetical citations. Dates are important for readers and researchers in the social sciences since so much of the research in psychology and related disciplines updates, builds upon, and corrects previous research.

The end-of-paper citations in APA style follow a pattern that, once learned, can be adapted easily to fit just about any desired work. Consult the accompanying chart of APA forms for an overview of the types of citations described in this section.

Directory of APA Sample In-Text, Parenthetical Citations

17a APA style for in-text, parenthetical citations

APA style uses two methods for citing borrowed material within the text: (1) Author and date are identified immediately following the borrowed material. (2) Author is identified in the text of the paper; the date is given immediately following the borrowed material. In-text, parenthetical citations provide readers with information needed to locate the source of borrowed information in the list of references at the end of the paper. In APA style, parenthetical citations identify what was borrowed from a source and when that source was published. Use the following guidelines when preparing parenthetical citations.

- Keep the citations concise, but provide all necessary information.
- Use an author's last name either in the text of the paper or in parentheses immediately after the borrowed material. Use an author's first initial and last name if two authors in the References share the same last name.
- Punctuate and format the parenthetical citations in the following manner.
    1. Place the parenthetical citation either at the end of the sentence or at a natural pause within the sentence. In either case, the citation should follow, as closely as possible, the material it refers to.
    2. If the citation is placed immediately following a quotation, place the citation after the closing quotation marks.
    3. Place any punctuation marks in the text immediately following the closing parenthesis of the citation.
    4. In block quotations, place the parenthetical citation two spaces following the final punctuation mark of the quotation.
- Include a page reference for the borrowed material.

1. Author not named in text

When an author is not identified in the text, place the author's last name and the year of publication in parentheses at a point where the citation does not interrupt the flow of your writing. Separate the author and date with a comma. Be sure that there is no confusion between what you are documenting and your own text.

```
During the Civil War, Thomas Carlyle supported the South,
but after the war he admitted that he might have been
wrong (Kaplan, 1983).
```

2. *Author named in text*

When an author is identified in the text, cite only the date within parentheses. If the same source is cited more than once in the same paragraph, you need not repeat the year in that and subsequent citations.

```
Kaplan (1983) analyzes Thomas Carlyle's admiration for
strong leaders like Cromwell and Frederick the Great.
```

In citing a direct quotation, include a parenthetical reference to the page number(s). The abbreviation *p.* or *pp.* is included.

```
"We are never innocent travelers; we arrive with ideas
about the place in our minds. These ideas may be more
vivid than the place can sustain when we see it; they
may be more resistant to change than the place itself"
(Howe, 1993, p. 62).
```

```
Howe (1993) has observed that "we are never innocent
travelers; we arrive with ideas about the place in our
minds" (p. 62).
```

3. *Work with two authors*

Always cite the surnames of both authors in all text citations. Use an ampersand (&) to separate the authors' names in a parenthetical citation, but use the word *and* to separate their names in the text of the paper.

```
The New Orleans Center for the Creative Arts has pro-
duced successful performers such as Wynton Marsalis and
Harry Connick, Jr. (Lichtenstein & Danker, 1993).
```

```
Lichtenstein and Danker (1993) demonstrate how the New
Orleans Center for the Creative Arts has produced suc-
cessful performers such as Wynton Marsalis and Harry
Connick, Jr.
```

4. *Work with three to five authors*

If a work has more than two but fewer than six authors, cite them all in the first reference.

```
The Tivoli in Copenhagen, one of the world's best-known
amusement parks, offers rides, games, fireworks, and
other attractions (Bendure, Friary, Noble, Swarey, &
Videon, 1993).
```

In subsequent references, however, cite only the first author followed by *et al.* (meaning "and others") neither italicized nor underlined.

```
According to Bendure et al. (1993), the Tivoli has no
peers.
```

5. Work with six or more authors

When a work has six or more authors, cite the surname of the first author followed by *et al.* in all in-text citations. Include the names of all the authors in the end-of-paper list of references. The following example shows a sample citation for a work by Rorschbach, Aker, Zorn, Flugel, Erskine, and Zieffer.

```
As Rorschbach et al. (1993) have suggested, the conse-
quences of radical demographic and cultural change on
midsize cities of the American heartland have yet to be
fully felt.
```

6. Anonymous work

Cite an anonymous work by using the first two or three words of the title in the in-text citation or parenthetically in place of the author's name.

```
While many questions about the Iran-Contra affair
persist, it seems unlikely any answers will be found
("Democracy," 1993).
```

7. Corporate author

Usually cite the full name of the corporate author in each in-text reference. If, however, the corporation's name is long or if an abbreviation for the company is easily recognized, abbreviate the corporate name in second and subsequent entries.

```
Recently published statistics show a decline in the
incidence of cerebral palsy (United Cerebral Palsy
Association [UCPA], 1994).
```

```
Governmental support for those with the disease cannot
be curtailed (UCPA, 1994).
```

8. Author of two or more cited works

In referring to two or more of the same author's works published in the same year, distinguish between them in the parenthetical citations by alphabetizing the works in the reference list and providing each work with a lowercase letter. Thus, Annette Kolodny's "Dancing through the Minefield" would be labeled *Kolodny, 1981a*, while her "A Map for Rereading" would be designated *Kolodny, 1981b*.

9. Authors with the same last name

To distinguish works by authors with the same last name, use each author's first initial(s) in each citation.

```
E. Jones (1930) wrote a pioneering study of psychology
and literature.
```

10. Two or more sources in a single citation

Cite two or more different authors in a single citation in alphabetical order and separated by a semicolon (Fetterley, 1978; Kolodny, 1975). Cite two or more works by the same author in a single citation in chronological order, separated by a comma (Flynn 1980, 1983).

11. Personal communication

Material such as letters, telephone conversations, messages from electronic bulletin boards, and personal interviews should be acknowledged in the text with the person's name, the identification *personal communication*, and the date. These sources are not included in the list of references because readers cannot retrieve them.

```
J. Holmes, president of Mayfair Fashions, predicts that
formal evening gowns will become more popular next year
(personal communication, December 29, 1993).
```

12. Web citations in text

When you cite material obtained from the Internet, use the same author/date format as you would for a print document. If you are citing a specific part of a Web document, provide the chapter, figure, or table. If you quote a Web document, give page or paragraph numbers if you have them.

17b APA style for the References list

APA style requires that all the sources of borrowed material in a paper be listed on a separate page at the end of the paper. This separate listing is called the "References." The References list should include only material that was used in the research and preparation of the paper.

Following the last page of the paper (but before any concluding notes or appendices) begin the list with the title "References" without quotation marks or underlining, centered, and an inch from the top of the page. The References list is paginated as the rest of the paper. Double-space between the title and the first entry on the list.

Arrange the citation entries in alphabetical order by authors' last names. If a source is anonymous, alphabetize it by using the first major word in its title (not *a*, *an*, or *the*). Begin each entry flush with the left margin, but indent all subsequent lines three spaces. Double-space within and between entries.

Books

A standard APA entry for a book consists of four elements: author, date of publication, title, and publication information. These four elements are separated from one another by a period. The entry concludes with a period. (Note that these formatting instructions are for preparing student papers. If you are submitting a paper to a journal for publication, refer to the *APA Publication Manual* for formatting guidelines.)

```
                    year of
                  publication
  ┌── author ─┐  ┌──────────┐  ┌──────── title ────────┐  ┌──
  Emerson, G.   (1976).   Winners and losers: Battles,
  ────────────────────── subtitle ──────────────────────
  retreats, gains, losses, and ruins from the
  ──────────────────────┐  ┌─ publication information ─┐
  Vietnam War.   New York: Norton.
  └── indent 3 spaces
```

Keep the following guidelines in mind when preparing book entries for the References list.

1. **Author:** An author's name should appear last name first, followed by a comma and first and middle initials. Put a period after the author's name.

2. **Year of publication:** Enclose the year of publication in parentheses and follow with a period.

3. **Title:** Underline the title and capitalize the first word of the title, the first word of the subtitle, and any proper nouns. Separate the main title from the subtitle with a colon. Put a period after the complete title.

4. **Publication information:** Include the city of publication and the publisher, separated from one another with a colon. If two or more locations are given for the publisher, either give the location that is listed first on the title page or give the site of the publisher's home office. If the name of the city is not well known or if it is confusing, include a state or country abbreviation following a comma. Omit the word *Publisher* and abbreviations such as *Inc.* and *Co.* from the publisher name. However, include the complete names of university presses and associations. Put a period after the publication information.

1. Book with one author

Emerson, G. (1976). Winners and losers: Battles, retreats, gains, losses, and ruins from the Vietnam War. New York: Norton.

2. Book with two or more authors

Bellah, R. N., Madsen, R., Sullivan, W., Swidler, A., & Tipton, S. M. (1985). Habits of the heart: Individualism and commitment in American life. Berkeley: University of California Press.

Lichtenstein, G., & Danker, L. (1993). Musical gumbo: The music of New Orleans. New York: Norton.

3. Book with an anonymous author

The world almanac and book of facts. (1983). New York: Newspaper Enterprise Association.

4. Book with an editor

Syrett, H. C. (Ed.). (1986). <u>The papers of Alexander
Hamilton</u> (Vol. 26). New York: Columbia University
Press.

5. Selection from an anthology

Chrisman, N. J. (1985). Alcoholism: Illness or disease?
In L. A. Bennett & G. M. Ames (Eds.), <u>The American
experience with alcohol: Contrasting cultural per-
spectives</u> (pp. 7-21). New York: Plenum.

6. Book with a corporate author

National Geographic Society. (1988). <u>Discovering
Britain and Ireland.</u> Washington, DC: Author.

7. Multivolume book

Cohen, J., & Chiu, H. (1974). <u>People's China and
international law: A documentary study</u> (Vols. 1-2).
Princeton: Princeton University Press.

8. Translation

Le Goff, J. (1980). <u>Time, work, and culture in the
Middle Ages</u> (A. Goldhammer, Trans.). Chicago:
University of Chicago Press.

9. Revised edition

Pauk, W. (1993). <u>How to study in college</u> (5th ed.).
Boston: Houghton Mifflin.

10. Republished book

Veblen, T. (1953). <u>The theory of the leisure class:
An economic study of institutions.</u> New York:
New American Library. (Original work published
1899)

11. Two or more books by the same author

Takaki, R. (1989). <u>Strangers from a different shore:
A history of Asian Americans.</u> Boston: Little,
Brown.

Takaki, R. (1993). <u>A different mirror: A history
of multicultural America.</u> Boston: Little,
Brown.

Gardner, H. (1982a). <u>Art, mind, and brain: A cognitive
approach to creativity.</u> New York: Basic Books.

Gardner, H. (1982b). <u>Developmental psychology</u> (2nd ed.).
Boston: Little, Brown.

12. Government publication

U.S. Department of Commerce. (1992). <u>U.S. industrial</u>
<u>outlook '92: Business forecasts for 350 industries.</u>
Washington, DC: U.S. Government Printing Office.

U.S. House of Representatives. Committee on Ways and
Means. (1986). <u>Hearings on comprehensive tax reform</u>
(Vols. 1-9). Washington, DC: U.S. Government Print-
ing Office.

Periodicals

A standard periodical entry in APA style includes the same
information as an APA standard book entry: author, date of publication, title, and publication information. These elements are
separated from one another by a period. The entry ends with
a period. (Note that these formatting instructions are for
preparing student papers. If you are submitting a paper to a
journal for publication, refer to the *APA Publication Manual* for
formatting guidelines.)

```
                    year of
                   publication
       ┌─ author ─┐ ┌───────┐ ┌──────────── title ───────────┐ ┌──────────
       Geertz, C. (1968). Thinking as a moral act: Dimensions
       ─────────────────────────── subtitle ───────────────────────────┐
       of anthropological fieldwork in the new states.
       ┌────── publication information ──────┐
       Antioch Review, 28, 139-158.
       └ indent 3 spaces
```

Keep the following guidelines in mind when preparing periodical entries for the References list.

1. **Author:** An author's name should appear last name first, followed by a comma, then by the first and middle initials.

2. **Year of publication:** Give the year of publication. For
   magazines and newspapers, include the month and date of
   publication. Enclose the year of publication information in
   parentheses and follow with a period.

3. **Title:** The article title and subtitle are neither underlined
   nor set in quotation marks. Capitalize the first word of the
   title, the first word of the subtitle, and any proper nouns.
   Separate the main title from the subtitle with a colon. Put a
   period after the title.

4. **Publication information:** Begin with the complete title of the
   publication, with all the major words capitalized. Underline
   the title. Provide the volume number (underlined and not
   preceded by the abbreviation *vol.*). End with the inclusive
   page numbers for the article. (APA includes the full sequence

of page numbers.) Use the abbreviation *p.* or *pp.* for articles in newspapers but not journals or magazines. Put a period at the end of the publication information.

13.   Article in a journal paginated by volume

Herzog, H. (1993). Human morality and animal research. American Scholar, 62, 337-349.

14.   Article in a journal paginated by issue

Livingston, H. (1980). Hamlet, Ernest Jones, and the critics. Hamlet Studies, 2(1), 25-33.

15.   Article in a magazine

Klaeger, R. (1986, November). Hiring the recent college grad. Video Manager, 14, 20.

16.   Article with an anonymous author

The talk of the town: Fanciers. (1990, December 31). The New Yorker, 28-29.

17.   Article in a newspaper

Claiborne, W. (1993, August 24). Boxes full of conspiracy? Researchers dig into JFK assassination papers. The Washington Post, pp. 1A, 7A.

18.   Editorial

Another tug-of-war over a child [Editorial]. (1993, September 7). The Chicago Tribune, p. 20.

19.   Letter to the editor

Deonarine, B. (1993, August). Basketball as a way out [Letter to the editor]. Harper's, 77-78.

20.   Review

Daynard, R. A. (1979). [Review of the book Watergate and the Constitution]. American Journal of Legal History, 23, 368-370.

Other Sources

21.   Abstract

Parked, K. R. (1992). Mental health in the oil industry: A comparative study of onshore and offshore employees. Psychological Medicine, 22, 997-1009. (From Psychological Abstracts, 1993, 80, Abstract No. 27688)

22. Published interview

Zunes, S. (1993, October). [Interview with George
    McGovern]. The Progressive, 34-37.

23. Dissertation

Etiegni, L. W. (1990). Wood ash recycling and land dis-
    posal. Unpublished doctoral dissertation, University
    of Idaho, Moscow.

When citing an abstract from *Dissertation Abstracts International
(DAI)*, do not underline the dissertation title. The words
Doctoral dissertation and the name of the university granting the
degree parenthetically follow the abstract title. Include the *DAI*
volume number, publication year, and page number.

Jenkins, D. J. (1993). Soldier theatricals: 1940-1945
    (Doctoral dissertation, Bowling Green State Univer-
    sity, 1992). Dissertation Abstracts International,
    53, 4133A.

24. Report

Jones, S. (1991). Traffic flow and safety in mid-size
    urban communities (Report No. TR-11). Albany: New
    York State Transportation Authority.

25. Film, television, or radio program

Scorsese, M. (Director), & DeFina, B. (Producer).
    (1993). The age of innocence [Film]. Hollywood:
    Columbia Pictures.

Shapiro, E. (Director), Clifford, T. (Producer), &
    Rather, D. (Anchor and Reporter). (1993, December 8).
    48 hours: State of fear. Boston: WHDH, CBS.

26. Videotape or videocassette

Keillor, G. (Narrator). (1992). The Dakota conflict
    (Videocassette No. 5790A). Botsford, CT: Filmic
    Archives.

Electronic Sources

The Publication Manual of the APA, fourth edition (1994),
contains few references to citing electronic sources, but the
APA has posted additional guidelines for the Internet and other
electronic sources on its Web page <http://www.apa.org/
journals/webref.html>. The formats are similar to those used
for print sources.

E-MAIL

E-mail is cited like other personal communications, such as letters. Because it cannot be retrieved by the reader, e-mail is not included in the list of references at the end of the paper. However, it is identified within the paper itself, as in this illustration.

```
According to I. M. Scofield (personal communication,
October 27, 1999), the project has been a success.
```

AN ENTIRE WEB SITE

To refer to an entire site (not a specific document on the site), a parenthetical citation in the text is sufficient, as in the following example. No reference entry is needed.

```
PsycPORT provides access to a wide variety of news
stories about psychology (http://www.psycport.com/).
```

SPECIFIC DOCUMENT ON A WEB SITE

Documents on a Web site are treated in much the same way as print documents. To cite Internet sources in APA format, (a) list complete information on author, date, title of article and/or larger work title, and pagination in the same format as for print sources. Then (b) provide the date you retrieved the document, followed by the complete URL. Preserve slashes, mechanics, and spaces within the address, without adding any final period. The first example is an article from an online version of a journal that contains all the information provided in its print equivalent. The second example comes from an online newspaper that does not have page numbers.

ARTICLE IN A JOURNAL

```
Parrott, A. C. (1999). Does cigarette smoking cause
    stress? American Psychologist, 54, 817-820.
    Retrieved October 29, 1999 from the World Wide
    Web: http://www.apa.org/journals/amp/
    amp5410817.html
```

ARTICLE IN A NEWSPAPER

```
Azar, B., & Martin. S. (1999, October). APA's Council
    of Representatives endorses new standards for
    testing, high school psychology. APA Monitor
    Online. Retrieved October 29, 1999 from the
    World Wide Web: http://www.apa.org/monitor/oct99/
    in1.html
```

17c APA manuscript format

SAMPLE APA TITLE PAGE

Relationships
1

Shortened title and page number

Intimate Relationships: A Review and
Analysis of Research in the Field
Rosette Schleifer

Title and author, centered

Psychology 201
Professor Robert Eisenberger
December 19, 1999

Course information if required

SAMPLE APA ABSTRACT

Relationships
2

Place abstract on a separate page; center heading

Abstract

Researchers over the last two decades have attempted to construct frameworks to account for the development of intimate relationships between humans. A review and analysis of this research suggest that no single framework or theoretical perspective adequately accounts for the complexity of intimate relationships; researchers interested in understanding the phenomenon must depend on a number of these frameworks rather than any single one.

Conclusion

Abstract summarizes subject, methods, findings, and conclusion

SAMPLE FIRST PAGE IN APA STYLE

Relationships
3

Intimate Relationships: A Review and
Analysis of Research in the Field

People tend to take the development of intimate personal relationships for granted. Trying to
understand these relationships based
exclusively on the nature of their intimacy (whatever that intimacy may indicate) can cause investigators to
ignore the evolutionary process that
leads to the formation of intimacy and
to the many factors that contribute to
its development. Focusing on development rather than on the fact of intimacy reveals how the level and depth
of relationships change over time and
how those changes are related to the
way in which the relationships developed in the first place. "Relationships develop in steps, not in slopes"
(Duck, 1988, p. 48).

Method

Over the last two decades, researchers have formulated a number of
theoretical frameworks to account for
intimacy in personal relationships.
This review of the work of eleven researchers focuses on whether any single framework provides a comprehensive
explanation of the nature of intimacy
in personal relationships and a sense
of just how intimacy develops.

Results

Several psychological processes
underlie the development of intimate
relationships. As these close relationships develop over time, several
changes take place as interaction between people increases and as partners
increase their investment in the relationship. In time, a sense of "WE-NESS"
develops (Perlman & Duck, 1987, p. 31).
Investigators trying to understand this

Annotations (left margin):
Introduction
presents an
overview of the
paper

Annotations (right margin):
Description
of how the
research was
conducted

Summary of
data collected
and how they
were analyzed

SAMPLE REFERENCES IN APA STYLE

APA-style reference list appears
on a separate page; heading is
centered

Relationships
6

References

Aron, A., Aron, E., Tudor, M., &
Nelson, G. (1991). Close relationships as including other in
the self. Journal of Personality
and Social Psychology, 60(2),
241-253.

Certner, B. (1973). Exchange of self-
disclosure in same sexed groups of
strangers. Journal of Counseling
and Clinical Psychology, 40(2),
292-297.

Cozby, P. (1973). Self-disclosure:
A literature review. Psychology
Bulletin, 79, 73-91.

Duck, S. (1988). Handbook of personal
relationships: Theory, research
and inventions. New York: Wiley.

Jourard, S. M., & Lasakow, P. (1958).
Some factors in self-disclosure.
Journal of Abnormal and Social
Psychology, 56, 91-98.

Pearlman, D., & Duck, S. W. (Eds.).
(1987). Intimate relationships:
Development, dynamics, and deteri-
oration. Newbury Park, CA: Sage.

Stephen, T. (1984). A symbolic exchange framework for the development of intimate relationships.
Human Relations, 37(5), 393-408.

Taylor, D. (1968). The development of
interpersonal relationships: Social
penetration processes. Journal of
Social Psychology, 75, 79-90.

Tierny, M. M. (1999). An intimate
look at Internet relationships.
Retrieved October 29, 1999
from the World Wide Web:
http://www.hightensionwires.com

VanLear, C., Jr. (1987). The formation
of social relationships: A long-
itudinal study of social penetration. Human Communication
Research, 13(3), 299-322.

Entries in
alphabetical
order, by
authors' name

Last names fir
initials only fo
first names

First line of ea
entry is flush
with left marg

Subsequent
lines of each
entry are
indented three
spaces

18

CMS Documentation Style

Many disciplines, including history, music and art history, philosophy, political science, economics, and business, use the citation system established by *The Chicago Manual of Style*, 14th edition (Chicago: University of Chicago Press, 1993), which features in-text numbered note references linked to endnotes describing the works cited, plus a bibliography for full reference details. Some instructors in other disciplines may prefer this system as well. You will likely encounter note and bibliography style in your research.

18a CMS bibliography entries

Format the bibliography as you would an MLA-style Works Cited list (see 16c). If you use footnotes, place your bibliography in the same place as you would a Works Cited list—after the last page of your paper. If you use endnotes rather than footnotes, place the bibliography after the page(s) of notes.

18b CMS endnotes or footnotes

Endnotes, which are placed together at the end of a paper, or **footnotes** at the bottom (or foot) of a page, provide publication information about sources you quote, paraphrase, summarize, or otherwise refer to in the text of a paper. When using the note system of documentation, place superscript numbers (raised slightly above the line—[1]) in the text of the paper. Place the number at the end of the sentence, clause, or phrase containing the material that you are documenting. Superscript numbers should be typed with no space between the letter or punctuation mark that precedes it. Number the citations sequentially throughout the paper. Each number will correspond to an entry in your footnotes or list of endnotes.

TEXT

As Janetta Benton has noted, gargoyles are usually located in "visually inaccessible locations,"[1] peripheral to the medieval cathedral. She also speculates that gargoyle sculptors can be compared with medieval

```
manuscript illuminators in their artistic freedom and
imaginativeness.²
```

NOTES

```
    1. Janetta Rebold Benton, The Medieval Menagerie:
Animals in the Art of the Middle Ages (New York:
Abbeville, 1992), 57.

    2. Benton, 58-59.
```

Use the following guidelines when writing with endnotes or footnotes.

- Place all endnotes at the end of the paper. Start a new page with the heading "Notes" (without underlining or quotation marks), centered and one inch from the top margin of the page. Double-space to the first note entry and between entries. This system is recommended by CMS and is widely preferred to footnotes.
- Place footnotes at the base of the page where the superscript number appears. The first line of the footnote begins four line spaces from the last line of text on the page. Single-space within a footnote, but double-space between footnotes.
- Indent each note five spaces from the left margin to the number. Follow the number with a period and one space. (Subsequent lines in an entry do not indent.)
- For the first occurrence of the standard note, begin the entry with the author's name in normal word order followed by a comma, the title of the source, the publication information in parentheses, followed by a comma and the page number(s).
- For the second and subsequent references to a source, use a shortened form of the entry consisting of the author's last name followed by a comma and the page number(s). When you use the shortened form of the entry for multiple citations to more than one work by the same author, include an abbreviated title in the entry.

Books

Book with one author

```
    1. Janetta Rebold Benton, The Medieval Menagerie:
Animals in the Art of the Middle Ages (New York:
Abbeville, 1992), 57.
```

Book with two or three authors

```
    2. Grace Lichtenstein and Laura Danker, Musical
Gumbo: The Music of New Orleans (New York: W. W. Norton,
1993), 124.
```

Book with more than three authors

3. Glenda Bendure et al., <u>Scandinavian and Baltic Europe on a Shoestring</u> (Berkeley: Lonely Planet, 1993), 26.

Book with an anonymous author

4. <u>The World Almanac and Book of Facts</u> (New York: NEA, 1983), 264-68.

Book with an author and an editor

5. George Orwell, <u>Orwell: The War Commentaries</u>, ed. W. J. West (New York: Pantheon, 1985), 210.

Book with an editor

6. Linda A. Bennett and Genevieve M. Ames, eds., <u>The American Experience with Alcohol: Contrasting Cultural Perspectives</u> (New York: Plenum, 1985), 15.

Selection from an anthology

7. Noel J. Chrisman, "Alcoholism: Illness or Disease?" in <u>The American Experience with Alcohol: Contrasting Cultural Perspectives</u>, ed. Linda A. Bennett and Genevieve M. Ames (New York: Plenum, 1985), 7-21.

Multivolume work

8. Joseph Blotner, <u>Faulkner: A Biography</u> (New York: Random House, 1974), 1:257.

Periodicals

Article in a journal paginated by volume

9. Adelia Williams, "Jean Tardieu: The Painterly Poem," <u>Foreign Language Studies</u> 18 (1991): 119.

Article in a journal paginated by issue

10. Daniel Bender, "Diversity Revisited, or Composition's Alien History," <u>Rhetoric Review</u> 12, no. 1 (1987): 115.

Article in a magazine

11. Bill Howard, "Portable Computing: Power without the Pounds," <u>PC Magazine</u>, August 1993, 254.

Article in a newspaper

12. William Claiborne, "Boxes Full of Conspiracy? Researchers Dig into JFK Assassination Papers," <u>Washington Post</u>, 24 August 1993, sec. A, pp. 1, 4.

Shortened Forms

Second and subsequent notes to the same source appear in a shortened form that lists the author's last name and page number only. Note that entries 14 and 15 show two works by the same author.

    13. Howard, 254.

    14. Benton, _Menagerie_, 145.

    15. Benton, "Perspective," 34.

CBE Documentation Style

The CBE styles of writing and documentation are described in _Scientific Style and Format: The CBE Manual for Authors, Editors, and Publishers_, 6th ed. (New York: Cambridge UP, 1994). Just as with MLA and APA styles of documentation, the CBE system includes both in-text, parenthetical citations and a list of end-of-paper references that contains more detailed bibliographic information about the sources cited. The CBE styles of in-text citation include the name-year system, which closely resembles APA style, and the citation-sequence system. This section explains and illustrates CBE in-text forms for both the name-year system and the citation-sequence system. The section also includes guidelines for preparing the CBE end-of-paper reference list.

19a   CBE style for in-text, parenthetical citations

The Name-Year System

To use the name-year system for in-text, parenthetical citations, provide the author's name and the publication year in parentheses. Do not separate author and date with a comma.

Edwin Hubble confirmed Heber Curtis's hypothesis that spiral nebulae are galaxies of stars (Ferris 1988).

If the author's name is mentioned in the text, use only the date in parentheses.

Ferris explains that Edwin Hubble confirmed Heber Curtis's hypothesis that spiral nebulae are galaxies of stars (1988).

To cite a work by an organization or agency when no author is listed, use the corporate or group name as the author.

The <u>Child Health Encyclopedia</u> notes that one infant in
a hundred is born with some type of heart defect (Boston Children's Medical Center 1975).

To distinguish between one of two or more works published by the same author in a single year, assign letters to the
books according to the alphabetical order of the titles' first major word (excluding *a*, *an*, or *the*). For example, to differentiate
between I. Bernard Cohen's *The Birth of the New Physics* and his
Revolution in Science, both published in 1985, cite the first book
as *Cohen 1985a* and the second as *Cohen 1985b*.

The Citation-Sequence System

The citation-sequence system for in-text, parenthetical citations involves using parenthetical arabic numerals to identify
the sources. This system has two variations. The *order-of-first-
mention* variation provides reference numbers for each work in
the order in which they appear in the paper and lists the full
citations in that order in the reference list. Alternatively, the
alphabetized variation allocates in-text reference numbers for
works as they appear in the alphabetized list of references at the
end of the paper.

ORDER OF FIRST MENTION
According to Gregory, Einstein drew on Planck's formula
as it was then used to describe oscillations of matter
(1). Once Einstein applied Planck's work to light, the
age of relativity, as Ferris (2) suggests, was born.

ALPHABETICAL ORDER
According to Gregory, Einstein drew on Planck's formula
as it was then used to describe oscillations in matter
(2). Once Einstein applied Planck's work to light, the
age of relativity, as Ferris (1) suggests, was born.

Whichever method you use, use it consistently and make sure
the in-text citations correspond in number to the references
listed at the end of the paper.

19b CBE style for the References list

The separate list of references that appears at the end of
the paper is the reference list. This list can be titled *References*
or *Cited References* and should be formatted much the same way
as the reference list described in the APA documentation style
(see 17b).

The arrangement of the entries in the reference list de-
pends upon the system of in-text citation used in the paper. If
the name-year system is used in the paper, arrange the entries

in the reference list alphabetically. Take care to double-space within and between items in the reference list and begin each entry at the left margin (any subsequent lines should indent three spaces). If either of the citation-sequence systems is used in the paper, each citation in the reference list will begin with the number used in the text. Follow the number with a period and two spaces to the entry (any subsequent lines should align on the first letter of the entry). (See 17b for how to organize the reference lists.)

Keep the following guidelines in mind when preparing book entries for the reference list.

1. **Number:** Assign a number to each entry only if a numbered in-text citation system is used.

2. **Author:** An author's name should appear last name first, followed by a comma and middle initials. Do not insert periods or spaces between initials. Put a period after the author's name. (Alphabetize the reference list by the author's last name if you are using the name-year system of in-text citation.)

3. **Title:** Capitalize the first word of the title and any proper nouns. Separate the main title from the subtitle with a colon. Put a period after the title.

4. **Publication information:** For a book, include the city of publication and the full name of the publisher, separated from one another with a colon. Put a semicolon after the publisher's name and provide the year of publication. Put a period after the publication year, followed by total number of pages for all book entries.

Books

The following citations are done in the citation-sequence format.

Book with one author

1. Ferris, T. Coming of age in the Milky Way. New York: Doubleday; 1988. 495 p.

2. Gregory, B. Inventing reality: physics as language. New York: Wiley; 1990. 230 p.

Book with two authors

3. Hazen, RM, Trefil, J. Science matters: achieving scientific literacy. New York: Doubleday; 1991. 294 p.

Book with a corporate author

4. Boston Children's Medical Center. Child health encyclopedia: the complete guide for parents. New York: Dell; 1975. 576 p.

Book with an editor

5. Held, A., editor. General relativity and gravitation.
    Volume 2, One hundred years after the birth of Albert
    Einstein. New York: Perseus Books, 1980. 558 p.

Periodicals

When citing periodical articles, keep the following in mind.

1. **Journal titles:** Abbreviate the title of the journal unless it is
    one word. Do not underline it. For example, the *Journal of
    Molecular Biology* would be abbreviated J. Mol. Biol.

2. **Publication information:** Provide the volume number (in
    arabic numerals) followed by a colon and the inclusive page
    numbers (without the abbreviations *p.* or *pp.*). For journal ar-
    ticles, conclude with a semicolon followed by the year of pub-
    lication and a final period.

Article in journal paginated by volume

6. Rickey, VF. Isaac Newton: man, myth, and mathematics.
    Coll Math J 1987; 18:362-89.

Article in journal paginated by issue

7. Eisenkraft, A; Kirkpatrick, L. Atwood's marvelous
    machines. Quantum 1993; 3(1):42-5.

Article in a newspaper

8. Stevens, WM. In new data on climate changes,
    decades, not centuries, count. New York Times 1993
    Dec 7; Sect C4 (col. 1).

Other Sources

Media sources

9. Kroopnick S. Treasures of the Titanic [Videocas-
    sette]. New York: Cabin Fever; 1988. VHS.

Computer disk

10. The New Grolier multimedia encyclopedia [CD-ROM
    program]. Danbury, CT: Electronic Publishing;
    1993. 2 MB RAM, 1 MB hard drive space, Microsoft
    Windows 3.1 with Multimedia Extensions 2.21.

Chart

11. Department of Communicative Disorders. Duluth:
    University of Minnesota. Hearing, language, social
    skills, motor skills [chart]; 1981.

For information about variations of these formats, consult
the *CBE Manual.* Also, see the accompanying chart that lists
style manuals you can refer to for additional information on
documenting sources in various disciplines.

Style Manuals in the Disciplines

Biology	*Scientific Style and Format: The CBE Manual for Authors, Editors, and Publishers.* 6th ed. New York: Cambridge UP, 1994.
Chemistry	Dodd, Janet S., ed. *The American Chemical Society Style Guide: A Manual for Authors and Editors.* Washington: ACS, 1985.
Education	National Education Association. *NEA Style Manual for Writers and Editors.* Rev. ed. Washington, DC: NEA, 1974.
General	Turabian, Kate L. *A Manual for Writers of Term Papers, Theses, and Dissertations.* 5th ed. Chicago: U of Chicago P, 1987.
	University of Chicago Press Editorial Staff. *The Chicago Manual of Style.* 14th ed. Chicago: U of Chicago P, 1993.
Law	Garner, Diane L., and Diane H. Smith. *The Complete Guide to Citing Government Information Resources: A Manual for Writers and Librarians.* Bethesda, MD: Cong. Info. Serv., 1993.
Languages and Literature	Gibaldi, Joseph. *MLA Handbook for Writers of Research Papers.* 5th ed. New York: MLA, 1999.
Mathematics	American Mathematical Society. *A Manual for Authors of Mathematical Papers.* Rev. 8th ed. Providence: AMS, 1990.
Physics	American Institute of Physics. *AIP Style Manual.* 4th ed. New York: AIP, 1990.
Psychology	*Publication Manual of the American Psychological Association.* 4th ed. Washington: APA, 1994.
Political Science	Kelley, Jean P., et al., eds. *Style Manual for Political Science.* Rev. ed. Washington: American Political Science Association, 1985.

part

4

Grammar

20
Verbs

A **verb** is a word or group of words that expresses the action or indicates the state of being of the subject of a sentence. Verbs activate sentences. Using verbs well will strengthen your writing.

20a Regular verbs

With the exception of the verb *be* and modal verbs such as *can* and *must*, regular English verbs have five forms.

Base Form	Present Tense	Present Participle	Past Tense	Past Participle
look	looks	looking	looked	looked
watch	watches	watching	watched	watched

A verb's *base form* is the form cited in dictionaries. It is used in present tense with *I, you, we, they*, or a plural noun. The base form is also used after *do* and following modal verbs such as *can* and *must*. (See 24g for modal verbs. For the important verb *be*, which does not conform to the normal pattern, see 24e.)

The present tense, or *-s* form, is used in the third-person singular—with *he, she*, or *it.*

The present participle, or *-ing* form, requires an auxiliary verb to make a complete verb phrase: *She was looking.*

The past tense, which uses *-d* or *-ed*, indicates completed action and does not require an auxiliary verb.

The past participle needs an auxiliary to form a complete verb phrase: *He was finished.* The past participle is used with a helping verb—*has, have*, or *had*—to form the perfect tenses: *She has worked; I have tried; we had ordered.* It is also used with *be, am, is, are, was, were, being*, or *been* to form the passive voice: *They were astonished; we had been surprised.*

Transitive and Intransitive Verbs Verbs can be transitive or intransitive. A **transitive verb** transfers its action from a subject to a direct object that completes its meaning:

➤ She *bought* the car. (The meaning of *bought* is completed by *car.*)

An **intransitive verb** does not need a direct object to complete its meaning.

➤ People *blush.* (The meaning of *blush* is complete in itself.)

Some verbs can be used both transitively (He *sees* his mistake) and intransitively (He *sees* poorly).

Linking Verbs   **Linking verbs** usually describe states of being, not actions. A linking verb joins the subject of a sentence to a subject complement, which describes or renames the subject.

➤ King Ferdinand *was* uncertain about Columbus's plan.

➤ Queen Isabella *felt* confident about Columbus's chances of success.

In these examples the verbs (*was, felt*) link their subjects (*King Ferdinand, Queen Isabella*) to the subject complements (*uncertain, confident*).

Common linking verbs include all forms of the verb *be* (*am, is, are, was, were, be, being,* and *been*). They also include sense verbs such as *sound, taste, smell,* and *feel:* The food *smells* and *tastes* delicious.

20b   Irregular verbs

Irregular verbs do not use -*d* or -*ed* to form the past tense and past participle. Examples include *began* and *gone*.

The following chart lists the most common irregular verbs. Additional irregular verbs can be found in a dictionary.

Common Irregular Verbs		
BASE FORM	**PAST TENSE**	**PAST PARTICIPLE**
arise	arose	arisen
awake	awoke	awaked *or* awoken
be	was	been
become	became	become
begin	began	begun
bite	bit	bitten
blow	blew	blown
break	broke	broken
bring	brought	brought
build	built	built
burn	burned *or* burnt	burned *or* burnt
burst	burst	burst
buy	bought	bought
can	could	could
catch	caught	caught
choose	chose	chosen
come	came	come
dig	dug	dug

(continued)

BASE FORM	PAST TENSE	PAST PARTICIPLE
dive	dived *or* dove	dived
do	did	done
draw	drew	drawn
drink	drank	drunk
drive	drove	driven
eat	ate	eaten
fall	fell	fallen
fight	fought	fought
fly	flew	flown
forget	forgot	forgotten *or* forgot
forgive	forgave	forgiven
get	got	gotten *or* got
give	gave	given
go	went	gone
grow	grew	grown
hang (suspend)	hung	hung
hang (execute)	hanged	hanged
have	had	had
hide	hid	hidden
know	knew	known
lay	laid	laid
lead	led	led
leave	left	left
lie	lay	lain
make	made	made
ride	rode	ridden
ring	rang	rung
rise	rose	risen
run	ran	run
see	saw	seen
set	set	set
shake	shook	shaken
shine (glow)	shone	shone
shine (polish)	shined	shined
shrink	shrank	shrunk
sing	sang	sung
sink	sank	sunk
sit	sat	sat
speak	spoke	spoken
spring	sprang	sprung
stand	stood	stood
steal	stole	stolen
stink	stank *or* stunk	stunk
swear	swore	sworn
swim	swam	swum
swing	swung	swung
take	took	taken
tear	tore	torn

BASE FORM	PAST TENSE	PAST PARTICIPLE
think	thought	thought
throw	threw	thrown
wear	wore	worn
write	wrote	written

Commonly Confused Irregular Verbs   Some verbs that are commonly confused are *sit* and *set, lie* and *lay, rise* and *raise*. *Sit, lie,* and *rise* are intransitive verbs and are not followed by a direct object. *Set, lay,* and *raise* are transitive verbs and are followed by a direct object. The following chart shows the forms of these frequently confused verbs:

Forms of *sit/set, lie/lay, rise/raise*					
	BASE FORM	PRESENT TENSE	PRESENT PARTICIPLE	PAST TENSE	PAST PARTICIPLE
Intransitive	sit	sits	sitting	sat	sat
Transitive	set	sets	setting	set	set
Intransitive	lie	lies	lying	lay	lain
Transitive	lay	lays	laying	laid	laid
Intransitive	rise	rises	rising	rose	risen
Transitive	raise	raises	raising	raised	raised

Sit means "to be seated"; *set* means "to put or place."

INTRANSITIVE: They *sat* against the wall. [past tense of *sit*]

TRANSITIVE: The explanation *set* her mind at rest. [past tense of *set*]

Lie is an intransitive verb and means "to recline." *Lay* is a transitive verb meaning "to put or place."

INTRANSITIVE: I often *lie* down after dinner. [present tense of *lie*]

TRANSITIVE: She *lays* down the law in our house. [present tense of *lay*]

INTRANSITIVE: I *lay* down before dinner last night. [past tense of *lie*]

TRANSITIVE: She *laid* the tray on my lap. [past tense of *lay*]

Rise is an intransitive verb and means "to get up." *Raise* is a transitive verb meaning "to lift up."

INTRANSITIVE: The foam was *rising* in the glass. [present participle of *rise*]

TRANSITIVE: They were *raising* their voices in celebration. [present participle of *raise*]

20c Verb tenses

Tense indicates when the action of a verb occurs, whether in the past, present, or future: *She wrote; she writes; she will write.*

These three tenses are called *simple tenses* to distinguish them from the *complex tenses:* the perfect, progressive, and perfect progressive tenses. The complex tenses indicate more complex relations of time than the three simple tenses of past, present, and future. A verb in one of the perfect tenses expresses an action that either has been completed or will be completed in relation to the time of another action. Perfect tense verbs are formed with *have* plus the past participle.

A verb in one of the progressive tenses expresses a continuing action. Progressive tense forms consist of a form of *be* plus the past participle.

The following chart shows the simple, perfect, and progressive tense forms for two verbs: *cook* and *eat.*

Verb Tenses		
VERB TENSES	**REGULAR VERB**	**IRREGULAR VERB**
Simple present	He *cooks*	She *eats*
Simple past	He *cooked*	She *ate*
Simple future	He *will cook*	She *will eat*
Present perfect	He *has cooked*	She *has eaten*
Past perfect	He *had cooked*	She *had eaten*
Future perfect	He *will have cooked*	She *will have eaten*
Present progressive	He *is cooking*	She *is eating*
Past progressive	He *was cooking*	She *was eating*
Future progressive	He *will be cooking*	She *will be eating*
Present perfect progressive	He *has been cooking*	She *has been eating*
Past perfect progressive	He *had been cooking*	She *had been eating*
Future perfect progressive	He *will have been cooking*	She *will have been eating*

Use the **present** tense:

- To designate a habitual action: I *exercise* every morning.
- To express a truth or a fact: Light *travels* faster than sound.
- To discuss works of literature and of art: Homer's *Odyssey* *is* a rousing adventure story. Frida Kahlo's self-portraits *reflect* her intense suffering.

Use the **present perfect** tense (*has* or *have* plus the past participle):

- To indicate that an action or its effects, begun in the past, continues into the present: She *has studied* foreign languages for many years.
- To indicate that an action of an unstated past time is related to the present: We *have traveled* extensively, so we are aware of cultural differences around the world.

Use the **present progressive** tense to indicate an action that is continuing in the present: We *are attempting* to resolve some thorny interpersonal conflicts.

Use the **present perfect progressive** tense to indicate actions that began in the past and continue into the present: Christine *has been running* her own business for more than twenty years.

Use the **past** tense to indicate action that occurred in the past and that does not extend into the present: Michael *worked* on his senior economics essay for two solid months.

Use the **past perfect** tense to indicate an action completed prior to another past action: The group *had sung* its last song when the lights went out.

Use the **past progressive** tense to indicate a continuing past action: They *were driving* through the mountains when they heard the news about the hurricane.

Use the **past perfect progressive** tense to indicate a continuing action that ended before another action: They *had been sending* relief supplies to Sarajevo when the United Nations curtailed the shipments.

Use the **future** tense to indicate actions that have not yet begun: Julia *will try* to get us free tickets.

Use the **future perfect** tense to indicate actions that will be completed at some future time: By the weekend, we *will have prepared* for the holidays.

Use the **future progressive** tense to indicate continuing action in the future: They *will be trying* for the third time to make the U.S. National rowing team.

Use the **future perfect progressive** tense to indicate a continuing action that will end in the future: In ten minutes, she *will have been jogging* for two hours.

Writing Hint   Always check your verb tenses when you edit and proofread your writing. Look at sentences where you have shifted tenses to ensure that those shifts are necessary. Avoid shifting between past and present tenses.

INCONSISTENT: The committee meeting *began* when the chair *calls* the members to order.

CONSISTENT: The committee meeting *began* when the chair *called* the members to order.

20d Verb mood

There are three moods for verbs in English: indicative, imperative, and subjunctive.

The **indicative mood** is used to state a fact, declare an opinion, or ask a question.

➤ Columbus *discovered* America. Columbus's discovery *requires* reexamination.

➤ *Did* Columbus really *discover* America?

The **imperative mood** (the base form of the verb with *you* understood as the subject) is used to give directions, orders, or advice.

➤ *Turn* left at the corner. *Send* this letter to Mrs. Chandler. *Study* chapters 7 through 10.

The **subjunctive mood** is used to express wishes, stipulate requirements, or make demands contrary to fact. Of these moods, the subjunctive is the most complicated. Use the following examples and the accompanying chart as a guide to using the subjunctive.

Uses of the Subjunctive
1. When expressing a wish: I wish he *were* more upset by what has happened. Gwen sometimes wished that her friends *were* still unmarried.
2. When expressing a state contrary to fact in an *if* clause: If the new medication *were* to be proven safe, many of the restrictions governing its use would be lifted.
3. When using clauses beginning with *as if* and *as though:* The captain of the football team acted as if he *were* a hero.
4. When expressing a demand, request, or recommendation in clauses beginning with *that:* The preacher suggested that she *make* a generous contribution. The position requires that all candidates *be* college graduates.

Writing Hint Avoid awkward shifting among the mood of verbs.

INCONSISTENT: *Drive* slowly on snowy roads and *you should keep* the car in lower gears than usual.

CONSISTENT: *Drive* slowly on snowy roads and *keep* the car in lower gears than usual.

20e Verb voice

Verbs can be in either the active or the passive voice. In **active voice,** the grammatical subject performs the action. In **passive voice,** what is done is emphasized over who performed the action.

Use the active voice to emphasize who or what performed an action: Michael *ate* the fudge royale ice cream. Use the passive voice to emphasize to whom or to what the action was directed: The fudge royale ice cream *was eaten* by Michael.

Verbs in the passive voice always include a form of the verb *be* immediately preceding the past participle of the main verb, as the accompanying chart indicates.

Active and Passive Voices		
VERB TENSES	**ACTIVE**	**PASSIVE**
Present	She *invites* us.	She *is invited.*
Past	She *invited* us.	She *was invited.*
Future	She *will invite* us.	She *will be invited.*
Present Perfect	She *has invited* us.	She *has been invited.*
Past Perfect	She *had invited* us.	She *had been invited.*
Future Perfect	She *will have invited* us.	She *will have been invited.*

Writing Hint   Maintain consistency in the voice of verbs. Avoid careless shifts between active and passive voice.

INCONSISTENT: The Japanese army *was being fought* in the Pacific while the Allies *defeated* the Germans at Normandy.

CONSISTENT: The American forces *were fighting* the Japanese in the Pacific while the Allies *were defeating* the Germans at Normandy.

20f Subject–verb agreement

In the present tense, a verb agrees with its subject in person (first, second, third) and in number (singular or plural.)

➤ A professional golf *tournament* usually *involves* four rounds of play.

The singular noun tournament takes a singular verb—*involves*. Note the characteristic third person *-s* ending (It involves).

Make Separated Subjects and Verbs Agree   Sometimes a subject and a verb are separated by other words or phrases.

➤ An *arrangement* of fresh flowers *arrives* at the house once a week.

➤ Low *scores* on the SAT may *discourage* you from applying to certain colleges.

Make Subject and Verb Agree with a Compound Subject   A **compound subject** is made up of two or more subjects joined by a conjunction. Compound subjects connected by *and* usually take a plural verb.

➤ Liberty, equality, and fraternity *have* long *been valued.*

However, when parts of a compound subject function as a single unit or refer to the same person or thing, the subject is considered singular, and the verb should also be singular.

➤ Ogilvy and Mather *is* known as a creative advertising agency.

With compound subjects connected by *or, nor, either . . . or,* or *neither . . . nor,* the verb may be singular or plural. When both parts of the subject are singular, the verb is singular.

➤ No food or drink *was* provided.

➤ Neither the referee nor the tournament director *knows* when play will resume.

When both subjects are plural, the verb is plural.

➤ Either the workers or the owners *need* to make concessions.

But when one part of the subject is singular and the other is plural, the verb agrees with the subject closer to it.

➤ To enroll, either junior standing or referrals from two faculty members *are* required.

Make a Verb Agree with an Indefinite Pronoun Subject   An **indefinite pronoun** does not refer to a specific person or thing. Most indefinite pronouns take a singular verb. (The accompanying chart lists common indefinite pronouns that take singular verbs.)

➤ Everybody *is* coming.

➤ Everyone who can help with the preparations *should* arrive early.

Indefinite Pronouns Taking Singular Verb Forms			
another	either	neither	other
anybody	everybody	nobody	somebody
anyone	everyone	no one	someone
anything	everything	nothing	something
each	much	one	

Some indefinite pronouns take plural verb forms: *both*, *few*, *many*, *others*, and *several*.

➤ Both *were* destroyed by the 1966 flood in Venice.

➤ Few, if any, *were* missed by the best students.

Still other indefinite pronouns can be either singular or plural, depending on the noun or pronoun they refer to: *all*, *any*, *enough*, *more*, *most*, *none*, and *some*.

SINGULAR: Some of the writing *is* excellent.

PLURAL: Some of the test questions *were* ambiguous.

Make a Verb Agree with a Collective Noun Subject A **collective noun** names a group of people or things. They include such words as *group*, *class*, *team*, *committee*, *herd*, *crowd*, *number*, *audience*, and *family*. Because collective nouns describe a group that is considered a single unit, they usually take singular verbs.

➤ The class *has performed* well throughout the term.

When emphasizing the individual members rather than the group as a whole, use a plural verb form.

➤ The jury *are* expected to return to their homes upon completing their work on the case. [The individual jury members will return to their own homes.]

Writing Hint Since use of a plural verb with collective nouns such as *committee* and *jury* may sound incorrect, you can add a prepositional phrase or a plural word such as *members* after the collective noun:
➤ The *committee members are* debating the proposal.
➤ The *herd of cattle cross* the river.

Make a Verb Agree with Its Subject Rather than a Complement Be sure a linking verb agrees with its subject and not with a complement.

➤ An important influence in politics today *is* minorities. [The verb, *is*, agrees with the singular subject *influence*, not with the plural complement *minorities*.]

However, if the parts in the last example were reversed, the verb would be the plural *are* rather than the singular *is*.

➤ Minorities *are* an important influence in politics today. [The subject is now *minorities*, which takes the plural verb *are*.]

Make a Verb Agree with Relative Pronoun Subjects

When the relative pronoun *who*, *which*, or *that* acts as the subject of a dependent clause, the verb in the clause must agree in number with the pronoun's antecedent.

➤ Success is the goal that *drives* many students to study hard. [*That* refers to *goal*, a singular noun, and takes the singular verb *drives*.]

➤ Success, self-satisfaction, and a desire to please one's parents are elements that *motivate* students to perform their best. [*That* refers to *elements*, a plural noun, and takes the plural verb *motivate*.]

When the phrase *one of the* comes before the relative pronoun, you need to check the intended meaning of the sentence.

➤ Cheryl is one of the team members who always *stay* late for extra practice. [Cheryl and some of her teammates stay late. *Who* refers to those who stay late for extra practice, and hence takes a plural verb.]

➤ Cheryl is the only one of the team members who *comes* to practice an hour early. [Only one player comes early—Cheryl. The antecedent of *who* is *one*, which takes a singular verb.]

Make Subject and Verb Agree in Inverted Sentences

In a sentence written with **inverted word order** (an inverted sentence), the subject follows the verb rather than precedes it. To maintain subject–verb agreement in inverted sentences, be sure that the verb agrees with the subject of the sentence, not with a nearby noun.

➤ Beneath the papers *was* the address book she had been looking for.

➤ Among the junk collected for the tag sale *were* a grandfather clock and an antique chair. [The compound subject is *a grandfather clock and an antique chair*, not *junk* or *sale*.]

Maintain Agreement with Singular Words that Appear Plural

Some nouns that look plural, such as *athletics*, *economics*, and *mumps*, are singular in meaning and take a singular verb.

➤ Athletics *is* an important source of revenue at many universities.

➤ Economics *predicts* the outcomes of some elections.

➤ Mumps *is* essentially a childhood disease.

Some nouns that look plural, such as *politics* and *statistics*, may be used as either singular or plural nouns under certain circumstances.

SINGULAR: Politics *fascinates* me. [*politics* is a field of study or a set of ideas]

PLURAL: His politics *are* very different from mine. [*politics* refers to beliefs or views]

Make Verbs Agree in Titles and with Words Used as Subjects Titles of books, films, and other works take a singular verb—even when those titles appear plural or contain plural words.

➤ "The American Geographies" *is* a wonderful essay written by Barry Lopez.

In the same way, a word referred to as a word takes a singular verb form, even though the word may be plural.

➤ The word "receivables" *is* used in business to mean an asset due to one business from another.

21

Pronouns

Pronouns take the place of nouns that precede or follow them in sentences. The noun that a pronoun refers to is called its **antecedent:** The doctor agreed to treat the *patient* only if *he* promised to follow the prescribed diet.

21a Pronoun case

Pronouns change form to reflect their function in a sentence. The grammatical role, or function, of a pronoun is indicated by its **case.** Pronouns may appear in the subjective, objective, or possessive case. The accompanying chart on the following page illustrates pronoun case forms.

Pronoun Case

Personal pronouns

Singular	SUBJECTIVE	OBJECTIVE	POSSESSIVE
First person	I	me	my, mine
Second person	you	you	your, yours
Third person	he, she, it	him, her, it	his, her, hers, its
Plural			
First person	we	us	our, ours
Second person	you	you	your, yours
Third person	they	them	their, theirs

Relative and interrogative pronouns

	SUBJECTIVE	OBJECTIVE	POSSESSIVE
	who	whom	whose
	whoever	whomever	

WRITING HINT   Avoid unnecessary shifts among first-, second-, and third-person pronouns.

INCONSISTENT: When *one* travels abroad, *you* should take traveler's checks instead of cash.

CONSISTENT: When *you* travel abroad, *you* should take traveler's checks instead of cash.

CONSISTENT: When *traveling* abroad, *take* traveler's checks instead of cash.

Case with Compound Structures   For compound subjects and objects, use the personal pronoun you would choose if the paired word and conjunction were not there. Use the accompanying chart to help you determine whether to use subjective or objective pronouns.

Deciding on Subjective or Objective Pronouns in Compound Structures

1. Separate each element of the compound structure.
   Bill and *she/her* attended the concert.
   Bill attended the concert.
   She attended the concert.
   I attended the concert with Amy and *he/him*.
   I attended the concert with Amy.
   I attended the concert with *him*.

2. Identify the case of the pronoun's function in the new
   sentence.

   She attended the concert. [*She* is the subject of *attended;* use
   the subjective.]

   I attended the concert with *him*. [*Him* is the object of *with*;
   use the objective case.]

3. Use the appropriate pronoun in the compound structure.

   Bill and *she* attended the concert.

   I attended the concert with Amy and *him*.

Case with Appositives   An **appositive** is a noun, noun
phrase, or pronoun that renames the noun or pronoun it immediately follows. A pronoun appositive takes its case from the
function of the noun it renames.

➤ The proposed wage increases, unfortunately, never included
   both groups of workers—the office staff and *us*. (The appositive renames *workers*, the object of the preposition *of*, so the
   objective case pronoun *us* is used.)

Case with Elliptical Constructions   An elliptical construction includes intentionally omitted words.

➤ I attend films more often than stage plays.

When such an elliptical construction ends with a pronoun, you
can mentally fill in the missing words to determine the grammatical function of the pronoun.

➤ My father has considerably more mechanical aptitude than *I*
   [have]. (*I* is the subject of the implied verb *have*.)

Using *we* and *us* with a Noun   You may occasionally use
the pronouns *we* or *us* before a noun to help establish the iden-
tity of the noun. If the noun is the subject or subject complement of a clause, use *we*.

➤ *We* athletes should stick together.

If the noun is an object, use *us*.

➤ They never bothered to consult with *us* students.

21b   *Who* and *whom*

Who and *whoever* are subjective forms used when the pronoun is the subject of a sentence or a clause. *Whom* and
whomever are objective forms used when the pronoun is the object of a verb or a preposition: *Who* proposed this new tax plan?
Whom will it benefit most?

In Questions You can decide whether to use *who* or *whom* at the beginning of a question by answering the question with a personal pronoun. If you can answer with a subjective case pronoun (*I, he, she we, they*), use *who* in the question. If you can answer with an objective case pronoun (*me, him, her, us, them*), use *whom*.

In Dependent Clauses Use *who* or *whoever* if the pronoun functions as the subject of the clause: Provide paper and pencils for *whoever* may need them. Use *whom* or *whomever* if the pronoun functions as an object in the clause: She was the candidate *whom* the electorate found most compelling.

You can use the accompanying charts to help you decide whether to use *who* or *whom* in questions and in dependent clauses.

Deciding When to Use *who* or *whom* in Questions

1. Ask the question with both forms of the pronoun.

   Who/Whom deserves the biggest bonus?

   Who/Whom should we recommend for promotion?

2. Answer the question with a personal pronoun.

   She deserves the biggest bonus. [Use the subjective personal pronoun.]

   We should recommend *him* for promotion. [Use the objective personal pronoun.]

3. Select *who* or *whom* based on the case indicated by the personal pronoun in your answer.

   Who deserves the biggest bonus?

   Whom should we recommend for promotion?

Deciding When to Use *who* or *whom* in Dependent Clauses

1. Identify the dependent clause.

   Many voters did not know *(who/whom) the minor party candidates were.*

   Most voters, however, know *(who/whom) the major candidates represent.*

2. Separate the subordinate clause, convert it to a statement, and choose a personal pronoun that fits the statement.

   They were the minor party candidates.

   The major candidates represent *them*.

3. Select *who* or *whom* based on the case of the appropriate personal pronoun.

   Many voters did not know *who* the minor party candidates were.

   Most voters, however, know *whom* the major candidates represent.

21c Pronoun reference

Make pronouns refer clearly to their antecedents. Avoid ambiguous, indefinite, or vague pronoun reference.

To avoid ambiguous reference, make a pronoun refer to a single antecedent.

CONFUSING: Grace told Diane she was not going. (The pronoun *she* could refer to either Grace or to Diane.)

CLEAR: Grace said that Diane was not going. Or: Grace told Diane to forget about going.

Avoid indefinite reference of the words *it* and *they*.

CONFUSING: In the introduction, *it* explains the author's thesis.

CLEAR: The introduction explains the author's thesis.

CONFUSING: In England, *they* serve tea in mid-afternoon.

CLEAR: Many people in England serve tea in mid-afternoon.

Avoid vague reference with the words this and that.

CONFUSING: The particle theory of light envisions light as composed of discrete particles or bits. The wave theory describes light as composed of larger units, which behave differently from particles. *This* was not understood until the early twentieth century. [What was not understood? The word *this* is vague.]

CLEAR: The particle theory of light envisions light as composed of discrete particles or bits. The wave theory describes light as composed of larger units, which behave differently from particles. *The differences between these theories* were not understood until the early twentieth century.

CONFUSING: Contrary to the beliefs of his contemporaries, Galileo theorized that the earth revolved around the sun. *That* earned him a severe reprimand from the Catholic Church. [There is no clear antecedent for *that*.]

CLEAR: Contrary to the beliefs of his contemporaries, Galileo theorized that the earth revolved around the sun. *Galileo's refusal to alter this belief* earned him a severe reprimand from the Catholic Church.

21d Pronoun–antecedent agreement

To avoid repeating nouns in writing, you can use pronouns to stand in for them. In doing so, however, be sure that each pronoun agrees with its antecedent in person, number, and gender.

➤ The cab *driver* cut through the traffic as if *he* were slalom skiing.

➤ Although *they* were placed in a glass case, the *trophies* meant nothing to her.

Make a Pronoun Agree with an Indefinite Pronoun Antecedent

An **indefinite pronoun,** such as *somebody* or *anything*, refers to an unspecified person or thing. Most indefinite pronouns are singular.

SINGULAR: *Everybody has* his or her opinion.

SINGULAR: If *someone is* guilty, he or she should confess.

Make a Pronoun Agree with a Collective Noun Antecedent

When a collective noun such as *team* or *class* refers to the group as a unit, the collective noun takes a singular pronoun.

➤ The class had to organize *its* own trip, without administrative assistance.

When a collective noun refers to the individual members of the group, it takes a plural pronoun.

➤ The group decided to split up and go *their* own different ways.

Make a Pronoun Agree with a Compound Antecedent

A **compound antecedent** has two antecedents joined by a conjunction. Compound antecedents can be either singular or plural. Those joined by *and* are plural and require a plural pronoun.

➤ The man and his dog took *their* daily stroll through the park.

When a compound antecedent is preceded by the word *each* or *every,* or if the sense of the compound is clearly singular—as when two words joined by *and* refer to a single person—use a singular pronoun.

➤ Oedipus's wife and mother, Jocasta, killed *herself* when she realized who Oedipus was and what he had done.

For compound antecedents connected by *or, nor, either . . . or,* or *neither . . . nor,* the pronoun should agree with the nearer of the two antecedents.

➤ Either the lead singer or the orchestra members must decide to follow *their* conductor's tempo directions.

Check for Gender-Specific Pronouns

Generic nouns and indefinite pronouns (such as *everyone* and *someone*) refer to both men and women, not to one sex or the other. Traditionally in English, when an indefinite pronoun or a generic noun served as the antecedent for a personal pronoun, that pronoun was the generic (or generalized) *he.*

➤ Did anyone neglect to bring *his* money for the trip?

➤ The person who organized this conference knew what *he* was doing.

Using the generic *he* in these examples, however, is sexist because it excludes women. The first example singles out males as most likely to forget their money. The second example assumes that the conference organizer must have been a male.

22
Adjectives and Adverbs

Adjectives and adverbs are modifers that describe, limit, or qualify other words. These modifiers add detail to writing and make it more vivid.

22a Adjectives

Adjectives modify nouns and pronouns.

➤ The *fearful* children entered the house.

Adjectives answer the questions *which*? *how many*? and *what kind*?

➤ The *yellow* crocuses were the *first* blooms of *last* spring.

Adjectives usually precede the words they modify, but they may also follow them.

➤ The *ripe and appealing* fruit sat on the counter.

➤ The fruit, *ripe and appealing,* sat on the counter.

Adjectives follow linking verbs such as *am, is, are, was,* and *were;* sense verbs such as *feel, smell, sound,* and *taste;* and verbs of becoming such as *become* and *grow.* When adjectives follow linking verbs they function as subject complements.

➤ The sauce *tasted* delicious. (Linking verb with an adjective modifying a noun.)

22b Adverbs

Adverbs modify verbs, adjectives, or other adverbs.

➤ *Yesterday,* we *anxiously* awaited word of her safe return.

Adverbs answer the questions *when*? (yesterday), *how*? (anxiously), *how often*? and *where*?

➤ Margaret, who sits *behind* me, *rarely* speaks up in class.

Adverbs can either precede or follow the words they modify.

➤ The waiter *carefully* set the dishes on the table.

➤ He worked *quickly*, without rushing.

22c Comparatives and superlatives

Adjectives and adverbs typically have three forms: positive, comparative, and superlative.

Positive	Comparative	Superlative
small	smaller	smallest
hungry	hungrier	hungriest
good	better	best
bad	worse	worst

The comparative form is used to compare two things; the superlative is used to compare three or more.

➤ Which of these two patterns do you like *better*?

➤ Who, in your opinion, is the *least* desirable candidate?

Adjectives of one and two syllables add *-er* and *-est* to form their comparative and superlative: *tough, tougher, toughest.* Longer adjectives use *more* and *most: dangerous, more dangerous, most dangerous.*

Avoid double comparisons, which use two comparative adjectives when only one is necessary.

FAULTY: Mozart's symphonies are *more better* known than his string quartets.

REVISED: Mozart's symphonies are *better* known than his string quartets.

Using *good/well* and *bad/badly*

Use the adjectives *good* and *bad* to modify nouns or pronouns: a *good* time; a *bad* play.

Use the adverbs *well* and *badly* to modify verbs, adjectives, or other adverbs: She speaks *well*; he hears *badly*. Note that *well* can be both an adjective and an adverb.

➤ He looked *well* when we last saw him, and he performed *well* during the competition. [The first is an adjective modifying *he*; the second is an adverb modifying *performed*.]

22d Misplaced modifiers

To be effective, modifiers, whether adjectives or adverbs, need to point clearly to the words and phrases they modify. Misplaced modifiers cause confusion for readers by being positioned in such a way that it is unclear what words they modify.

CONFUSING: Ten doctors play golf at the hospital.

CLEAR: Ten doctors at the hospital play golf.

CONFUSING: Ann was unhappy that she failed to win the contest by a large margin.

CLEAR: Ann was unhappy that she failed by a large margin to win the contest.

Interrupting Modifiers Modifying phrases and clauses that come between a subject and verb can be awkward and confusing.

AWKWARD: The concert, because it snowed heavily all day, was canceled.

REVISED: Because it snowed heavily all day, the concert was canceled.

Modifiers that split parts of a verb phrase can also cause awkwardness and confusion.

AWKWARD: Many television viewers will, when it is time for a commercial, change channels or get something to eat.

REVISED: When it is time for a commercial, many television viewers will change channels or get something to eat.

Squinting Modifiers A modifier that appears to refer to the words before and after it is said to squint. Revise squinting modifiers by moving them so it is clear what they modify.

SQUINTING: The man who spoke quickly ran out of breath.

REVISED: The man who quickly spoke ran out of breath.

REVISED: The man who spoke ran quickly out of breath.

22e Dangling modifiers

A modifier is said to dangle when it does not modify any word or phase in a sentence.

DANGLING: As a small child, Sally's mother used to tell her bedtime stories.

REVISED: When Sally was a small child, her mother used to tell her bedtime stories.

DANGLING: When sunny, Kristie's spirits are as bright as the day.

REVISED: When the day is sunny, Kristie's spirits are bright.

23

Sentence Boundary Problems: Fragments and Run-ons

When sentence boundaries are not clear, readers can easily become confused. The two primary kinds of sentence boundary errors are fragments and run-ons.

23a Sentence fragments

A **sentence fragment** is an incomplete sentence that is punctuated as a sentence. To be a sentence, a group of words must contain an independent clause with a subject and verb, and it must be able to stand alone. To repair fragmented sentences, you can either turn the fragment into a sentence by adding words, or you can connect the incomplete sentence fragment with adjoining words to form a complete sentence.

Phrase Fragments   A *phrase* is a group of words that lacks a subject, a verb, or both subject and verb. A phrase misused as a sentence is called a *phrase fragment*. Correct phrase fragments in one of the following ways:

1. Attach the phrase to an independent clause.

   FRAGMENT: The Gore welfare proposal required a tax increase. For the middle class.

   REVISED: The Gore welfare proposal required a tax increase for the middle class.

2. Make the phrase into an independent clause by adding a subject, a verb, or both.

   FRAGMENT: Music held many attractions for Bach. Particularly the opportunity for religious expression.

   REVISED: Music held many attractions for Bach. He particularly valued the opportunity it afforded for religious expression.

Clause Fragments   A dependent clause looks much like a sentence, with a subject and a verb. It begins with a subordinating word, such as *although, because, if, unless,* which suggests that the clause cannot stand alone as a sentence. Revise dependent clause fragments in one of the following ways:

1. Combine it with an independent clause either before or after it.

   FRAGMENT: Much of the country watched. As the Denver Broncos won the Super Bowl.

REVISED: Much of the country watched as the Denver Broncos won the Super Bowl.

2. Convert the clause fragment into an independent clause.

FRAGMENT: Because the band's performance was well attended.

REVISED: The band's performance was well attended.

Relative Pronoun Fragments One of the most common kinds of sentence fragment begins with a relative pronoun such as *who*, *which*, or *that*. Be careful to avoid fragments such as the following:

FRAGMENT: They hoped to win the lottery. Which would solve their financial problems.

REVISED: They hoped to win the lottery, which would solve their financial problems.

FRAGMENT: They wanted to see the new film. That they had read about.

REVISED: They wanted to see the new film that they had read about.

Acceptable Fragments Writers sometimes use fragments for emphasis. Advertisements often contain fragments for emphasis.

➤ American Playhouse. The film festival in your living room. Only on PBS.

Unless you are striving for an informal tone, avoid fragments in academic and professional writing.

23b Run-on sentences

Run-on sentences are incorrectly joined or fused independent clauses. Two or more independent clauses occurring within a sentence must be joined by appropriate punctuation, either a period or a semicolon.

There are two kinds of run-ons: fused sentences and comma splices. A **fused sentence** runs two or more sentences together without any punctuation between them. A **comma splice** joins two sentences with a comma, where a period or semicolon is necessary.

FUSED SENTENCE: Beethoven was not born deaf he lost his hearing gradually.

COMMA SPLICE: Beethoven was not born deaf, he lost his hearing gradually.

REVISED: Beethoven was not born deaf. He lost his hearing gradually.

REVISED: Beethoven was not born deaf; he host his hearing gradually.

Sometimes fused sentences and comma splices can be corrected by adding a coordinate or a subordinate conjunction. (Coordinate conjunctions—*and, or, nor, for, but, yet, so*—join parallel words, phrases, or clauses. Subordinate conjunctions—*because, if, unless, although, until*—indicate the relationship of the dependent [or subordinate] to the main clause of a sentence.)

FUSED SENTENCE: I finally found the film it was not what I expected.

REVISED, COORDINATE CONJUNCTION: I finally watched the film, but it was not what I expected.

REVISED, SUBORDINATE CONJUNCTION: When I finally watched the film, it was not what I expected.

COMMA SPLICE: They were close to their destination, they kept walking.

REVISED, COORDINATE CONJUNCTION: They were close to their destination, *so* they kept walking.

REVISED, SUBORDINATE CONJUNCTION: *Since* they were close to their destination, they kept walking.

Note: You can also use conjunctive adverbs such as *however, moreover, furthermore, therefore,* and *nevertheless,* to join clauses.

REVISED, CONJUNCTIVE ADVERB: They were close to their destination; therefore, they kept walking.

Notice the punctuation surrounding the conjunctive adverb *therefore:* a semicolon before and a comma following.

Writing Hint   Conjunctive adverbs increase the formality of writing. Overuse of the conjunctive adverb can slow writing down because the semicolon needed before it creates a longer pause than does a comma.

➤ She did not plan to major in economics, but she did.

➤ She did not plan to major in economics; however, she did.

24

Special Concerns for ESL Writers

If English is not your native language, you may find some of its features troublesome. A few aspects of English to focus on are nouns and their accompanying articles (*a, an,* and *the*), sentence word order, and verb forms (especially of *be, have,* and *do,* and modal auxiliaries).

24a Count nouns and noncount nouns

A *count noun* refers to people, places, or things that are counted separately. Count nouns may be singular or plural.

➤ Twenty-two *students* signed up for English 101.

➤ One *student* never came to class. She was a transfer *student*.

A *noncount noun* is a noun that cannot be counted separately, such as *air*, *water*, and *wealth*. Noncount nouns do not have a plural form.

➤ The *light* in the lecture hall was dim, and the *air* was pleasantly cool. Haroun had little *sleep* the night before.

Do not use *a* or *an* or a number before noncount nouns.

INCORRECT: We had *a rice* for dinner.

INCORRECT: We had *rices* for dinner.

REVISED: We had *rice* for dinner. *It* was delicious.

Words that indicate measures or portions can be used to show plural quantities of noncount nouns.

➤ He ate *three bowls* of rice for dinner.

➤ Please pick up *two pounds* of chicken at the supermarket.

➤ The movers left *a few pieces* of furniture on the sidewalk.

24b Using articles correctly

English has two kinds of articles: the **indefinite articles** *a* and *an* and the **definite article** *the*. In deciding whether to use *a*, *an*, or *the*, you must first determine whether the noun is indefinite or definite. A noun is indefinite when neither the writer nor the reader has a specific person, place, or thing in mind.

➤ Let's try to find *a parking place*. [any parking place, not a specific one]

➤ Could we open *a window*? [any one of several windows]

➤ I love *music*. [music in general]

A noun is **definite** when both the writer and the reader know which specific person, place, or thing it refers to.

➤ Where is *the parking lot*? [a specific lot]

➤ I opened *the window*. [the only window]

➤ I love *the music* of the Jazz Age. [a particular style of music]

Next, determine whether the noun is a noncount noun or a count noun. Use the accompanying chart on the following page to decide on how to assign articles to count and noncount nouns.

Choosing the Correct Article		
NOUN TYPE	**IF INDEFINITE**	**IF DEFINITE**
Singular count noun cat, hour	Use *a* or *an*	Use *the*
Plural count noun cats, hours	Use no article	Use *the*
Noncount beauty, time	Use no article	Use *the*

Using *a* or *an* with Singular Count Nouns   Use *a* or *an* with every indefinite singular count noun.

INCORRECT: I wore *hat* today.

REVISED: I wore *a hat* today.

Every singular count noun must be preceded by a determiner. If the context does not require *a* or *an*, use another determiner.

INCORRECT: We found *suitcase*.

REVISED: We found *a suitcase*.
We found *the suitcase*.
We found *our suitcase*.

Writing Hint   Use *a* before a consonant sound. Use *an* before a vowel sound. Note that it is the initial sound, not whether the first letter is a consonant or a vowel, that determines whether *a* or *an* should be used.

➤ *a* delicious meal; *a* history examination

➤ *a* unique painting; *a* university [the *u* is pronounced like the consonant *y*]

➤ *an* appetizer; *an* umbrella

➤ *an* honest waiter; *an* hour later [the *h* is silent]

Using *the*   You can use the definite article *the* with all nouns—singular count nouns, plural count nouns, and noncount nouns. The accompanying box indicates when to use *the*.

When to Use the Definite Article *the*

- Use *the* when the noun has been mentioned previously. After the noun has been introduced, the reader knows which person, place, or thing it refers to.

   Early one morning, *a* child wandered into the Fifth Precinct station on Manhattan's Lower East Side. *The* child was shoeless and seemed to be lost. [*The child* was described in the preceding sentence.]

- Use *the* when the person, place, or thing is unique or generally known.

   The weather is getting stranger every year. [There is only one phenomenon we refer to as the weather.]

I have never seen *the* Grand Canyon. [There is only one Grand Canyon.]

Many immigrants pursue *the* American Dream. [The concept is generally known.]

- Use *the* when the context makes it clear which person, place, or thing is being referred to.

The sick baby is crying. [There is one sick baby.]

The flowers on your desk are beautiful. [There is one arrangement of flowers on the desk.]

- Use *the* when a clause or an adjective limits the noun so that it is clear which one is being referred to.

Schindler's List was the best movie I saw in 1993. [There can only be one *best* movie.]

- You can use one *the* for two or more nouns joined by *and*.

Dan circled *the* correct answer. [There is only one possible correct answer.]

People congregated on *the* porch and deck.

Insects flew amid *the* flowers, trees, and shrubs.

Using Plural Count and Noncount Nouns without an Article   Do not use an article with plural count nouns or with noncount nouns when you make a generalization. A **generalization** is a statement based on or a conclusion derived from a limited number of examples.

INCORRECT: *The friends* are important.

REVISED: *Friends* are important.

INCORRECT: *The love* makes the world go around.

REVISED: *Love* makes the world go around.

24c   Using correct word order

Use the accompanying chart to determine typical word order when you use two or more descriptive adjectives.

Word Order of Adjectives and Other Noun Modifiers

1. **Determiner:** *a, an, the, these, those, your, their, Sue's, anyone's, many, a few, a little, some, too much, too many*

2. **Words indicating order or number:** *first, initial, second, next, final, last, one, twenty*

3. **Adjectives expressing opinion or judgment:** *easy, attractive, dedicated*

4. **Adjectives indicating size or length:** *small, large, tall, long, short*

(continued)

5. **Adjectives indicating shape or width:** *round, square, circular, oval, wide*

6. **Adjectives indicating condition:** *broken, dilapidated, smooth-running*

7. **Adjectives indicating age:** *old, young, new, modern, antique*

8. **Adjectives indicating color:** *blue, green, yellow, aquamarine, amber*

9. **Adjectives indicating nationality or religion:** *Spanish, Chinese, Muslim*

10. **Adjectives indicating material:** *plastic, stone, wood*

11. **Nouns used as adjectives:** *dining room, student*

12. **The noun**

Examples:

| 1 | 2 | 6 | 11 | 12 |

Those last warm summer nights in September remind me of my childhood.

| 2 | 4 | 5 | 10 | 11 | 12 |

Six large oval mahogany kitchen tables were delivered to the wrong house.

| 1 | 3 | 9 | 12 |

A number of remarkable Italian restaurants can be found in Boston's North End.

| 1 | 12 | 1 | 3 | 7 | 8 | 12 |

My brother refurbished that sleek vintage green Mustang.

24d Distinguishing between present participles and past participles used as adjectives

Both the **present participle,** such as *irritating* and *pleasing,* and the **past participle,** such as *irritated* and *pleased,* can function as adjectives in a sentence. When used as adjectives present and past participles have very different meanings. Participles that describe feelings or states of mind can be troublesome for nonnative speakers, as the following examples illustrate.

INCORRECT: I was *embarrassing*.

REVISED: I was *embarrassed* by his behaviors. [the past participle used as an adjective]

REVISED: It was an *embarrassing* moment for me. [the present participle used as an adjective]

INCORRECT: It was an *interested* film.

REVISED: It was an *interesting* film. [the present participle used as an adjective]

REVISED: The *interested* audience did not speak during the showing of the film. [the past participle used as an adjective]

Keep the following in mind when you use participles as adjectives.

- Use present participles (*boring, intriguing, fascinating, exhilarating*) to describe people, places, or things that *cause* a feeling or state of mind:

  The book was *thrilling*. [The book caused this feeling.]

  New York is an *exhausting* city. [The place causes this feeling.]

- Use past participles (*bored, intrigued, fascinated, exhilarated*) to describe people, places, or things that *experience* that feeling:

  Kyung Hua is *fascinated* by English. [She experiences a feeling of fascination.]

  The tourists will be *exhausted* by noon. [They will experience exhaustion.]

- Take special care when using the following participles:

Present Participles	**Past Participles**
amazing	amazed
annoying	annoyed
boring	bored
depressing	depressed
exciting	excited
exhausting	exhausted
fascinating	fascinated
frightening	frightened
interesting	interested
satisfying	satisfied
surprising	surprised

INCORRECT: Kyung Hua was *surprising* by her parents' arrival.

REVISED: Kyung Hua was *surprised* by her parents' arrival.

INCORRECT: *The Grapes of Wrath* offers a *fascinated* view of life during the Great Depression.

REVISED: *The Grapes of Wrath* offers a *fascinating* view of life during the Great Depression.

24e   Learning the forms of *be, have,* and *do*

The verbs *be, have,* and *do* are used frequently, both as main verbs and as auxiliary verbs. Since they are irregular, you must memorize their forms.

Remember that all English sentences require a main verb. Do not omit the verb in a sentence that has a complement, a word that describes the subject.

INCORRECT: He late.

REVISED: He *was* late.

INCORRECT: They never wrong about prices.

REVISED: They *are* never wrong about prices.

Keep in mind the changes required for third-person singular forms of *be*, *have*, and *do*. Use the accompanying chart for reference.

Forms of *be*, *have*, and *do*				
BASE FORM	**PRESENT TENSE**	**PRESENT PARTICIPLE**	**PAST TENSE**	**PAST PARTICIPLE**
be	I *am* he/she/it *is* we/you/they *are*	*being*	I/he/she/it *was* we/you/they *were*	*been*
have	I *have* he/she/it *has* we/you/they *have*	*having*	I *have* he/she/it *had* we/you/they *had*	*had*
do	I *do* he/she/it *does* we/you/they *do*	*doing*	*did*	*done*

24f Using the auxiliary verbs *be, have,* and *do* correctly

The **auxiliary verbs** (also called **helping verbs**) *be*, *have*, and *do* combine with a base form or a participle to create a verb phrase.

➤ As a child I *was told* to study.

➤ I *have learned* a lot about national politics this year.

➤ I *do know* about the surprise party.

Progressive tenses, perfect tenses, the passive voice, negatives, and questions are all formed with auxiliaries.

Progressive Tenses The **progressive tense** is used to indicate an action that continues in the past, the present, or the future. Use the appropriate form of *be* and the present participle to create the progressive tenses.

Remember the following points when you use the progressive tenses.

- The form of *be* must agree with the subject.

    INCORRECT: Bob *are going* to class even though he feels sick.

    REVISED: Bob *is going* to class even though he feels sick.

- Do not omit a form of *be* with the progressive tenses.

    INCORRECT: *We starting* a new school club.

    REVISED: *We are starting* a new school club.

Some verbs are used rarely in the progressive. They occur in the following categories. You must learn which verbs they are to use them correctly.

LINKING VERBS
be, become, exist, seem

VERBS THAT SHOW POSSESSION
belong, have, own, possess

VERBS THAT SHOW PERCEPTION
feel, hear, see, smell, taste

VERBS THAT SHOW FEELINGS, PREFERENCES, AND INTELLECTUAL STATES
believe, forget, hate, imagine, intend, know, like, love, need, pity, prefer, remember, suppose, understand, want, wish, wonder

INCORRECT: That book *is belonging* to Yokari.

CORRECT: That book *belongs* to Yokari.

Perfect Tenses   The **perfect tense** is used to indicate an action that has been completed before another action begins, or an action finished by a specific time. Use the appropriate form of *have* and the past participle to create the perfect tenses.

➤ Akiko *has visited* the United States three times. [This sentence uses the present perfect tense to indicate that her visits began and ended sometime in the past. In the present perfect, the past participle of the main verb follows the present of *have*.]

➤ She *had wanted* to visit the Deep South last February, but visited Australia instead. [This sentence uses the past perfect tense to indicate that she wanted to travel to the Deep South sometime before she went to Australia. In the past perfect, the past participle of the main verb follows the past participle of *have*.]

Remember the following points when you use the perfect tenses.

- The form of *have* must agree with the subject.

    INCORRECT: My brother *have seen* every Clint Eastwood movie.

    CORRECT: My brother *has seen* every Clint Eastwood movie.

- Do not omit a form of *have* when you use the perfect tenses.

  INCORRECT: Professor Lewis *gone* on sabbatical.

  CORRECT: Professor Lewis *has gone* on sabbatical.

- Use the past participle of the main verb, not the past tense, to form the perfect tenses.

  INCORRECT: Abdul and Sara *have ran* in the Boston marathon several times.

  CORRECT: Abdul and Sara *have run* in the Boston marathon several times.

When you are not sure how to form the past participle, check your dictionary. If the past participle and the past tense have different forms, the dictionary will give both forms.

Usage Note   The present perfect tense after *since* requires a specific time. The present perfect after *for* requires a span of time.

➤ We have been visiting this campground *since 1989*.

➤ We have been visiting this campground *for ten years*.

Passive Voice   In the **passive voice,** the grammatical subject of a sentence receives the action of the verb. Use the passive voice when the subject is unknown or considered relatively unimportant.

➤ My brother *was elected* class president. [The emphasis in this sentence is on *My brother* rather than those who elected him.]

The passive voice combines the past tense of *be* and the past participle. Keep the following points in mind when you use the passive voice.

- The past participle never changes, but the auxiliary *be* must agree with the subject.

  INCORRECT: Many home-based businesses *was created* in the 1980s.

  CORRECT: Many home-based businesses *were created* in the 1980s. [The auxiliary *were* agrees with the plural subject *businesses*.]

- Use only transitive verbs in the passive voice. Transitive verbs, such as *kiss* and *hit*, are verbs that take a direct object.

  ACTIVE: Brazilians *speak* Portuguese.

  PASSIVE: Portuguese *is spoken* by Brazilians.

- Intransitive verbs, such as *smile* and *occur,* do not take an object. They cannot be used in the passive voice.

INCORRECT: A strange thing *was happened* yesterday.

REVISED: A strange thing *happened* yesterday.

24g   Modal auxiliaries

A **modal auxiliary** is an auxiliary verb that is used with a main verb to indicate necessity, obligation, permission, or possibility.

➤ Wang *should wear* a suit to his interview tomorrow.

➤ They *might offer* him the job.

Modals give information about the speaker or writer's attitude toward that verb. Modals have only one form. The accompanying chart indicates how to use modals.

	Using Modals	
MODAL	**MEANING CONVEYED**	**EXAMPLE**
can, could	ability	Carla *can* run five miles. I *could* run last year, but I *cannot* run today.
should	advisability	It is going to rain. You *should* take an umbrella.
must, have to	necessity	We *must* remember to go to the library. We *have to* return some books.
not	prohibition	You *must not* park in front of the police station.
must, must not	logical necessity	This letter *must* be from Svetlana. I know no one else in Moscow. The Smiths *must not* know our new telephone number.
will, would	intention	I think I *will* go to the movies tomorrow.
may, might, could	possibility	Fred is sick. He *may* or *may not* come to the meeting today.

Keep the following in mind when you use modals in your writing.

• Do not use the third-person singular *-s* ending with a modal.

INCORRECT: Glen *musts* register soon, or he will not get into the class.

CORRECT: Glen *must* register soon, or he will not get into the class.

- Always use the base form of the verb, not the infinitive or past tense, after a modal.

  INCORRECT: Sid and Maria *could to speak* English last year.

  INCORRECT: Sid and Maria *could spoke* English last year.

  CORRECT: Sid and Maria *could speak* English last year.

- When the modal is followed by another auxiliary verb (*be, have,* or *do*), use the base form of the auxiliary verb. (See 24e–f for more on forms of *be, have,* and *do*.)

  INCORRECT: The package *could not been delivered.*

  REVISED: The package *could not be delivered.*

- Do not use more than one modal with any main verb. Use one of the following phrases as a substitute for the second modal.

Modal	Substitutes
can	be able to
must	have to
should	supposed to, be obliged to

  INCORRECT: Sylvia *might can* pass the history test this semester.

  CORRECT: Sylvia *might be able to* pass the history test this semester.

- Use the perfect tense after *could, would,* and *should* to relate something that did not happen. Do not substitute *of* for *have* in this structure.

  INCORRECT: I *could of* worked last summer, but I decided to attend summer school instead.

  CORRECT: I *could have* worked last summer, but I decided to attend summer school instead.

Writing Hint Modal auxiliaries can combine with other auxiliary verbs to form complicated verb phrases that require careful attention.

When *have* comes after a modal auxiliary, as in "I could have gone," the *could have* is pronounced with stress on *could* and no stress on *have.* Thus, in speech *could have* sounds like *could of* and is sometimes incorrectly written that way. Be sure to write *have,* not *of,* in this type of sentence.

➤ You *should have read* the directions more carefully.

➤ It *would have saved* you considerable time and energy.

25
Conciseness

In academic and professional writing, your first goal should be clarity. You want to be understood. You can achieve clarity through correct grammar and punctuation. But clarity is enhanced with conciseness and emphasis, which we discuss here.

Conciseness involves saying what you have to in only as many words as necessary. To achieve conciseness, use the following guidelines.

Eliminate unnecessary words. Avoid redundancy, the needless repetition of words and phrases, such as *true facts* and *future hope*. Be careful to avoid redundant verbs such as *join together* and *refer back*.

Replace empty phrases such as *at the present time* (now), and *give consideration to* (consider). Such empty phrases are formulaic and inflated. Use the shorter, simpler alternative for each of the following empty phrases.

Wordy	Concise
Due to the fact that	because
For the most part	mostly
In close proximity to	near
In spite of the fact that	although
In the event that	if
Aware of the fact that	know

Avoid negating words. Instead of writing "I do not approve," write "I disapprove." Instead of "He is not feeling well," write "He is ill."

Avoid excessive use of the verb be. Forms of *be*—*is, are, am, was, were, been*, and *being*—may be associated with wordiness. Sentences with multiple forms of *be* can almost always be trimmed.

WORDY: It *is* sometimes the case that students *are* absent from class when assignments *are* due.

CONCISE: Students sometimes miss class when assignments are due.

Use active verbs. Active voice verbs invigorate writing by emphasizing action. Sentences with active voice verbs tend to be shorter than those with passive voice verbs.

PASSIVE: It has been decided that an increase in tuition will be instituted next semester.

ACTIVE: The Board of Trustees decided to increase tuition next semester.

Besides being more concise, the active voice version provides more specific information: it tells *who* made the decision to increase tuition.

Prefer verbs to nouns. The tendency to use nouns rather than verbs is called *nominalization*. Noun-heavy sentences can become abstract and devoid of energy. Instead of writing "We will make a recommendation," write "We will recommend." Instead of "The judge will give a ruling on the issue," prefer "The judge will rule on the issue." Put the emphasis on the act.

Eliminate unnecessary intensifiers. Some intensifiers, such as *very* and *really*, can usually be cut. If something is *very likely possible*, it is *probable*. If someone is *very, very tired*, he is *exhausted*. Such intensifiers actually diminish rather than intensify the words they modify.

26
Emphasis

Writing concisely helps achieve **emphasis.** Emphasis involves stressing your most important ideas, key words, and phrases. The following guidelines will help you write more emphatically.

Emphasize through deliberate, purposeful repetition. In writing about Martin Luther King, Jr., Alice Walker uses repetition to emphasize his contributions.

➤ He gave us back our heritage. He gave us back our homeland [. . .]. He gave us the blueness of the Georgia sky in autumn [. . .]. He gave us continuity of place [. . .]. He gave us home.

And James Baldwin uses a kind of double repetition with variation in this sentence about his father.

➤ It had something to do with his blackness, I think—he was very black—with his blackness and his beauty, and with the fact that he knew that he was black but did not know that he was beautiful.

Emphasize through short sentences. When used with longer sentences, short sentences can be emphatic. Ralph Waldo Emerson begins a long paragraph in his essay "Self-Reliance" with this sentence: "Trust thyself." And Thoreau, in *Walden*, follows a series of long sentences with this one-word sentence: "Simplify!"

Emphasize through inversion. By inverting the order of the standard subject–verb–object, you can achieve emphasis. In the following sentence, E. B. White uses inversion three times.

➤ Out of its wild disorder comes order; from its rank smell rises the good aroma of courage and daring; out of its preliminary shabbiness comes the final splendor.

White's sentence about the circus emphasizes *order, courage and daring,* and *splendor.* Each comes at the end of a clause. But *splendor* is most heavily emphasized because it comes last, the most emphatic position in a sentence.

Emphasize through parallelism. Parallelism involves using similar grammatical structures to coordinate words, phrases, and clauses both within and between sentences.

PARALLEL WORDS: Life's necessities include food, clothing, and shelter.

PARALLEL PHRASES: With malice toward none, with justice for all . . .

PARALLEL CLAUSES: There is a time for joy; there is a time for sorrow.

Use parallel structures as often as possible, to coordinate items in a series to the more elaborate parallelism of phrases, clauses, and sentences. The British writer and thinker Francis Bacon uses parallel structure to good effect in sentences such as these.

➤ Some books are to be tasted, others to be swallowed, and some few to be chewed and digested.

➤ Read not to contradict and confute; nor to believe and take for granted; nor to find talk and discourse; but to weigh and consider.

27

Appropriate Words

To write well, you need to use the right words, those that best convey your meaning with clarity, conciseness, and emphasis. The right words, however, are not always easy to find, and en route to finding them, writers sometimes use words that impede rather than enhance their meaning.

27a General and specific, abstract and concrete words

General words identify broad categories (*country, president, books*); **specific words** identify individual people or objects

(*Thailand, president of the AFL-CIO, dictionaries*). **Abstract words** identify ideas and ideals that cannot be perceived by the senses (*education, generosity, fatherhood*); **concrete words** identify something tangible to the senses (*rose, stone, tomato*). Good writing uses words from both ends of the spectrum, from abstract and general words to concrete and specific ones. Abstract and general terms represent ideas, explain attitudes, and explore relationships such as contingency (if something will happen), causality (why it occurs), and priority (what is first in time or importance). Concrete and specific words clarify and illustrate general ideas and abstract concepts. Successful writers typically alternate between abstract and concrete words and general and specific language, blending them naturally.

To achieve this mix, use abstract and general words to state your ideas. Use specific and concrete words to illustrate and support them.

GENERAL/ABSTRACT
➤ Technology revolutionized communication in the 1990s.

SPECIFIC/CONCRETE
➤ The invention of cellular phones made mobile phone conversations possible.

Notice how the language used in the second sentence creates a more focused image than does that of the first sentence. The following examples, which build on the first two sentences, focus the idea more because the language becomes more and more specific and concrete.

GENERAL/ABSTRACT
➤ Industrialists with cellular phones have meetings from their cars.

SPECIFIC/CONCRETE
➤ Donald Trump uses his cellular phone to make business deals from the back seat of his limousine.

27b Formal and informal language

Formal language represents the standard or level of discourse suitable for academic and professional writing. The tone of formal language is serious without being stuffy or pretentious. Formal language adheres to the conventions of standard English, including rules of grammar, sentence structure, and punctuation.

Colloquialisms, informal expressions appropriate to ordinary spoken language, are not acceptable in academic and professional writing. Expressions such as *hang out with* and *put a spin on* should be avoided.

Slang should also be avoided. Most slang words go out of fashion in a few years, anyway. *Far out* and *geek* have been displaced by other "cool" terms. Using slang in conversation is fine. That's where it belongs. But avoid it in serious writing.

Jargon is the specialized or technical language of a trade, profession, or other group. When doctors talk of treating a patient's viral rhinorrhea with a salicylate, most patients would not know that their common cold was being relieved with aspirin. When communicating among members of a specialized group, jargon is acceptable. But when you are writing for or speaking to a more general audience, you should avoid jargon, even the jargon of computerspeak with its hackers and viruses, or you will not be understood, which is, after all, the first principle of communication.

Dialect expressions—language that uses regional variations in grammar, vocabulary, and spelling—may also have a place in informal communication. In academic and professional communication, though, take pains to avoid nonstandard dialect and regional forms of expression, such as "I reckon I'll get on my way" and "I'm right sorry about that."

> **Writing Hint** Follow the general guideline of consistency with regard to the formality or informality of tone you establish in a piece of writing. Shifts in language and tone from formal to informal language can be disconcerting to readers.
>
> **INCONSISTENT:** Columbus's voyages continue to spark debate, with some scholars out to trash the Italian mariner's reputation.
>
> **CONSISTENT:** Columbus's voyages continue to spark debate, with some scholars providing a critical reinterpretation of the Italian mariner's reputation.

27c Biased language

Be careful to avoid biased language, which disparages, stereotypes, or patronizes others. Biased language typically reflects negative assumptions about sex, race, or ethnicity. Referring to women as "girls," to Native Americans as "Indians," and to Italian Americans as "wops" are just a few of the many ways bias and insensitivity appear in language. Be sure to use forms of reference preferred by the groups to which you refer.

Avoid using the word *man* or *men* to refer to both women and men. Also avoid words containing those terms, such as *congressman* and *man-made* (use *legislator* and *synthetic* instead).

SEXIST: It is time for all good *men* to stand up and be counted.

REVISED: It is time for all good *people* to stand up and be counted.

SEXIST: The *congressmen* should vote against the proposal.

REVISED: The *legislators* should vote against the proposal.

Avoid "feminine" suffixes such as *-ess* and *-ette*.

SEXIST: Rita Dove is a prominent American *poetess*.

REVISED: Rita Dove is a prominent American *poet*.

Use parallel terms when referring to members of both sexes. Do not always put the male term first as if it were the more important.

SEXIST: Dr. Noel Rogers and Linda Rogers have been *man and wife* for ten years.

REVISED: Noel and Linda Rogers have been *husband and wife* for ten years.

Instead of *men and ladies,* say *ladies and gentlemen* or *men and women.*

Use plural forms instead of singular masculine forms.

SEXIST: A *doctor* must work as an intern and resident before *he* can be licensed to practice medicine independently.

REVISED: *Doctors* must work as interns and residents before *they* can be licensed to practice medicine independently.

Eliminate the pronouns entirely.

REVISED: *A doctor* must work as an intern and resident before *being* licensed to practice medicine independently.

Avoid using gender terms unnecessarily, as with *male nurse* or *female lawyer.*

SEXIST: The *male nurse* was represented by three *women lawyers*.

REVISED: The *nurse* was represented by three *lawyers*.

Avoid using language that patronizes either sex.

SEXIST: His response to a crisis is *womanish*.

REVISED: His response to a crisis is *ineffectual*.

27d Other kinds of biased language

Avoid language and expressions that show insensitivity toward age, religion, social class, geographical location, and sexual orientation.

- *Age* A young person may resent being called an *adolescent,* while an older person may not wish to be described as *elderly* or *senior.*
- *Religion* Keep your language free of judgmental words concerning a person's religion. Avoid overgeneralization by implying that all Catholics have big families, that all

Protestant Christians can quote scripture, or that all Muslims wear turbans and speak Arabic.

- *Social Class*   Avoid disparaging social terms such as *redneck*, *white trash*, and *wealthy snob*. Remember that your audience may come from across the social spectrum.
- *Geographical Area*   Avoid stereotyping people based on where they live or grew up. Not all New Yorkers are rude, nor do they all live fast-paced lives. Southerners do not all speak with a drawl, and not all Californians are surfers and sun lovers.
- *Sexual Orientation*   Do not assume that your readers share your sexual orientation any more than they may share your political views or religious beliefs. Avoid referring to a person's sexual orientation unless it is relevant. In discussing the acting career of Rock Hudson, for example, mention his homosexuality only if it is relevant to your point.

28

Varied Sentences

To achieve a readable style, make sure there is variation in your sentences. Vary the length of your sentences. Remember that a short sentence coming after a few longer ones can be emphatic. Vary the kinds of sentences you write, mixing in an occasional question or inversion. Vary the ways you begin your sentences. Avoid beginning every sentence with a noun or pronoun (or with its accompanying article: *a*, *an*, or *the*).

The following paragraph about alcohol illustrates some of these forms of sentence variety.

> I still shy away from nightclubs, from bars, from parties where the solvent is alcohol. My friends puzzle over this, but it is no more peculiar than for a man to shy away from the lions' den after seeing his father torn apart. I took my own first drink at the age of twenty-one, half a glass of burgundy. I knew the odds of my becoming an alcoholic were four times higher than for the children of nonalcoholic fathers. So I sipped warily.
>
> —Scott Russell Sanders, "Under the Influence"

Now examine another paragraph from the same essay, in which the author uses a short sentence in the middle as a transition to bridge the two parts of his paragraph.

The secret bores under the skin, gets in the blood, into the bone, and stays there. Long after you have supposedly been cured of malaria, the fever can flare up, the tremors can shake you. So it is with the fevers of shame. You swallow the bitter quinine of knowledge, and you learn to feel pity and compassion toward the drinker. Yet the shame lingers and, because of it, anger.

One of the easiest ways to check sentence openings for variety is to circle the first two or three words of each sentence. You will quickly see whether your sentences begin the same way with monotonous consistency. You can also count the words in your sentences to check for variety in the length of your sentences. Of course, when you discover a lack of variety, you then have to introduce more varied sentences into your revised draft.

Use the accompanying checklist to help you avoid the tedium of too many sentences of similar length.

Checking for Varied Sentence Length

- Count the words in each sentence.
- If many sentences are the same length (within five words), rewrite some to vary their lengths.
- Look at strings of short sentences to see if they should be combined to express more clearly the relationship between their ideas.
- Look at your longest sentences to see if any contain more than a single idea. Consider splitting such sentences to better emphasize their different ideas.

29
Confusing Sentences

Occasionally you may write sentences that confuse readers. Some of the more common pitfalls to avoid are sentences with mixed grammatical constructions, incomplete comparisons, and faulty parallelism.

Mixed Sentences   Avoid beginning with one grammatical pattern and switching to another mid-sentence.

MIXED CONSTRUCTION: After hearing so many conflicting views was the reason we became confused.

This confused sentence can be revised in a number of ways:

REVISED: After hearing so many conflicting views, we became confused.

REVISED: Hearing so many conflicting views confused us.

REVISED: The many conflicting views confused us.

Writing Hint Mixed sentences often result from careless use of an introductory phrase or clause.

MIXED: In walking briskly for twenty minutes is a good aerobic exercise.

REVISED: Walking briskly for twenty minutes is good aerobic exercise.

Incomplete and Inconsistent Comparisons Incomplete comparisons leave out words, phrases, or clauses that are essential for meaning, thus cresting ambiguity.

INCOMPLETE COMPARISON: Peg's dedication was greater.

REVISED: Peg's dedication was greater than ours.

REVISED: Peg's dedication was greater than ever before.

INCONSISTENT COMPARISON: Victoria likes classical music better than Joan.

Does she like classical music better than she likes Joan, or does she like classical music better than Joan does?

Faulty Parallelism Avoid mixing different grammatical structures when listing items in a series, whether single words, phrases, or clauses.

FAULTY PARALLELISM: The vacation package included food, lodging, recreation, and having entrance fees paid for.

REVISED: The vacation package included food, lodging, recreation, and entrance fees.

part

6

Punctuation and Mechanics

Commas

Commas help readers understand writers' sentences. Although comma use may vary somewhat among writers, the following situations require using one or more commas.

30a Before a coordinating conjunction that links independent clauses

Use a comma to separate two independent clauses when the second clause is preceded by a coordinating conjunction (*and, but, or, nor, for, so, yet*). An independent clause is a group of words that can stand alone as a sentence. The comma signals the end of one independent thought and the beginning of another.

➤ The forces of repression have reemerged, yet the people's thirst for freedom has not been quenched.

If the clauses are short, the comma may be omitted.

➤ I played well but I did not win.

30b After an introductory word or word group

Use a comma after an introductory word, expression, phrase, or clause. The comma indicates that the introductory word group has come to an end and that the main part of the sentence is beginning.

➤ Reluctantly, he agreed to the deal.

➤ In a reversal of opinion, the committee approved the proposal.

➤ After the Oscars had been awarded, ticket sales for winning films soared.

➤ To explain his military decision, the president made a nationally televised speech.

You may omit the comma after short introductory elements if doing so does not cause confusion.

➤ After class we should meet for lunch.

30c Between items in a series

Use commas to separate items in a series of three or more words, phrases, or clauses.

> He did not know whether the car was a Ford, a Buick, or a Chevrolet.

Some writers prefer to omit the comma before the last item in a series. It is never wrong to put a comma there, and omitting it can sometimes cause confusion.

30d Between coordinate adjectives

Use a comma to separate coordinate adjectives (adjectives that modify the same noun or pronoun).

> The job required careful, patient, methodical work.

Do not use commas between adjectives that do not each modify the noun separately.

> The dark blue fabric appealed to them. [Dark modifies blue, not fabric.]

30e To set off nonrestrictive elements

Words, phrases, and clauses that constitute **restrictive elements** of a sentence limit the meaning of the words they modify and are not set off from the main clause of the sentence with commas. **Nonrestrictive elements,** which do not limit the meaning of the words they modify, are set off from the main clause of a sentence with commas.

RESTRICTIVE: Professional athletes *who perform exceptionally* deserve their high salaries.

NONRESTRICTIVE: Bobby Bonds, *who led the league in home runs and batting average*, deserves his high salary.

In the first example, the clause *who perform exceptionally* is essential to the meaning of the sentence since it restricts the meaning of *professional athletes.* The modifying clause is thus not set off by commas. In the second example, the clause *who led the league in home runs and batting average* does not limit the noun it modifies, *Bobby Bonds.* Instead, it provides additional information about him. It is therefore nonrestrictive and is set off with commas. Restrictive elements, especially clauses and participial phrases, usually identify the noun they modify: *who perform exceptionally* identifies which athletes deserve high salaries. The clause modifying the noun *Bobby Bonds* does not identify or restrict the noun to a greater degree.

Sometimes a modifying element can be interpreted as either restrictive or nonrestrictive. Your use of commas, or no commas, will tell the reader what you intend. Consider how the punctuation changes the meaning of the following sentence.

➤ The houses, needing a coat of paint, were given one.

➤ The houses needing a coat of paint were given one.

The first sentence suggests that all the houses needed a coat of paint. The second sentence implies that only some houses needed a coat of paint.

> **Writing Hint** You can decide whether to set off an element with commas by imagining your sentence without the words in question. If the words can be deleted without altering the meaning of the sentence or without confusing its meaning, they are nonrestrictive and should be set off with commas. If they cannot be deleted without altering sentence meaning, they are restrictive and should not be set off with commas.
>
> ➤ The major computer manufacturers, which have been battling for control of the U.S. market, have begun a series of joint ventures. [The clause *which have been battling for control of the U.S. market* adds incidental information about the major computer manufacturers but does not identify them. Removing the clause would not change the basic meaning of the sentence; the clause is nonrestrictive.]
>
> ➤ The companies that stand to lose the most are manufacturers of software. [The clause *that stand to lose the most* defines which companies are being talked about. Removing the clause would make the sentence almost meaningless; the clause is therefore restrictive and should not be separated by commas.]

Nonrestrictive Adjective and Adverb Clauses A clause that functions as an adjective or an adverb in a sentence can be either restrictive or nonrestrictive. Only nonrestrictive clauses are set off with commas.

NONRESTRICTIVE CLAUSES

➤ The American political system, *although it has faults*, remains one of the finest in the world. [The clause is not necessary to the meaning of the independent clause and is therefore nonrestrictive.]

➤ I borrow books from my local public library, *which has a splendid collection of material on animals*. [The clause is not essential to the meaning of the independent clause and is thus set off with a comma.]

RESTRICTIVE CLAUSES

➤ Every approach *that the group thought reasonable* was tried. [The clause restricts the meaning of *Every approach*. Dropping the clause would change the meaning of the sentence.]

Writing Hint When you write sentences that include relative clauses, use *that* only for restrictive clauses. Some writers use *which* for both restrictive and nonrestrictive clauses, although many prefer to use *which* only for nonrestrictive clauses.

Nonrestrictive Phrases Both participial and prepositional phrases can be either restrictive or nonrestrictive, though prepositional phrases are usually used restrictively.

NONRESTRICTIVE PHRASES

➤ Nicole and Pierre, *pleased with their first game*, decided to play another.

➤ Marilyn Monroe, *even with all the adulation she received*, was unhappy.

RESTRICTIVE PHRASES

➤ Money received *as a gift* is not as special as money earned.

➤ The tray *for the dessert* is on the top shelf.

Nonrestrictive Appositives An **appositive** is a noun or noun substitute that replaces another noun or noun substitute by renaming it. Those appositives that are nonessential to the meaning of what they rename are set off with commas.

NONRESTRICTIVE APPOSITIVES

➤ Raymond Carver, *one of contemporary America's best short-story writers*, never published a novel.

➤ Michelangelo's *David*, *a sculpture carved from an enormous block of Carrera marble*, is approximately eighteen feet high.

RESTRICTIVE APPOSITIVES

➤ The American writer *Ernest Hemingway* once remarked that all of modern American literature derived from Mark Twain's *The Adventures of Huckleberry Finn*. [*Ernest Hemingway* identifies which American writer made the remark.]

30f To set off transitional and parenthetical expressions

Transitional expressions bridge sentences or parts of sentences. They include conjunctive adverbs, such as *therefore* and *however*; and phrases such as *for example*.

➤ On the other hand, it should not have been so surprising.

When a transitional expression occurs between independent clauses, it is preceded by a semicolon and is usually followed by a comma.

➤ Jesse did not complete the take-home final exam; moreover, she missed the midterm as well.

Parenthetical expressions add supplementary information and are not essential to the structure of the sentence.

➤ It was, in fact, an amazing discovery.

30g To set off absolute phrases and contrasting elements

An **absolute phrase** modifies an entire independent clause.

➤ The game over, the fans headed for the exit ramps.

Contrasting elements require separation with commas.

➤ The children, not the adults, had the best roles.

30h To set off direct address, *yes and no,* and tag questions

➤ Friends, Romans, countrymen, lend me your ears.

➤ No, that will not be an acceptable form of payment.

➤ It was not a successful film adaptation, was it?

30i To set off direct quotations

➤ Of Montaigne's essays Emerson said, "Cut these words and they bleed."

30j With dates, addresses, and titles

Dates
➤ The book was published on August 30, 1999, and released on January 1, 2000.

Commas are not necessary if the date is inverted, or if only month and year are given.

➤ The book was published on 30 August 1999 and released in January 2000.

Places
➤ Dover, Delaware, bears little resemblance to Dover, England.

Titles
➤ Lucia Hernandez, Ph.D., is the youngest historian on the faculty.

30k Misuses of the comma

Avoid using unnecessary commas in the following situations:

Between compound elements that are not independent clauses.

NOT: He was elected unanimously, and immediately assumed the position.
BUT: He was elected unanimously and immediately assumed the position.

Between subjects and verbs.

NOT: The jubilant crowd, welcomed the victorious team home.
BUT: The jubilant crowd welcomed the victorious team home.

Between restrictive elements.

NOT: Jane Austen's novel, *Pride and Prejudice*, is a classic.
BUT: Jane Austen's novel *Pride and Prejudice* is a clsssic.

After a coordinating conjunction.

NOT: Most *Seinfeld* episodes were taped but, the last episode was live.
BUT: Most *Seinfeld* episodes were taped, but the last episode was live.

Before *than*.

NOT: Attending the party after the show was more exciting, than the show itself.
BUT: Attending the party after the show was more exciting than the show itself.

After *like* or *such as*.

NOT: Computer add-ons, such as, printers and software, increase the cost.
BUT: Computer add-ons, such as printers and software, increase the cost.

Before a clause beginning with *that*.

NOT: It was clear, that a storm was coming.
BUT: It was clear that a storm was coming.

Before a parenthesis.

NOT: There were only three candidates, (all middle-aged men) for the position.
BUT: There were only three candidates (all middle-aged men) for the position.

To set off an indirect quotation.

NOT: Who was it who first said, that truth lies in the eye of the beholder?

BUT: Who was it who first said that truth lies in the eye of the beholder?

31

The Semicolon

Semicolons are used to separate sentence elements, usually independent clauses; they are also used to separate items in a series that contains internal punctuation.

31a Between independent clauses

Use a semicolon to signal a close relationship between independent clauses. Use the semicolon in place of a comma and coordinating conjunction when the relationship between the clauses is clear.

➤ The train gathered speed; the brakes squeaked; it lurched and stopped.

—Paul Theroux, *The Great Railway Bazaar*

31b Between independent clauses and a conjunctive adverb or a transitional phrase

Independent clauses joined by conjunctive adverbs—*however, moreover, therefore*—require a semicolon between them.

➤ They expected the concert to be boring; however, they found it engaging.

Transitional phrases such as *as a result* and *on the other hand* are preceded by a semicolon following an independent clause.

➤ The president's approval rating dropped ten points; as a result, the White House stepped up its media blitz.

31c Between items in a series containing internal punctuation

Use semicolons to separate items in a series in which internal commas are present.

➤ The course objectives included understanding the basic tenets of Hinduism, Buddhism, Confucianism, Islam, Judaism, and

Christianity; appreciating the cultural beliefs associated with these religious philosophies; and recognizing the diverse ways the world's peoples acknowledge the divine.

31d Misuses of the semicolon

Do not use the semicolon in the following situations:

Between a subordinate clause and the rest of the sentence.

NOT: Until you think through the organization of a paper or report; writing an outline won't be much help.

BUT: Until you think through the organization of a paper or report, writing an outline won't be much help.

Between independent clauses joined by a coordinating conjunction when neither clause contains internal commas.

NOT: Only three of them knew the game; but all were willing to play.

BUT: Only three of them knew the game, but all were willing to play.

Between an independent clause and a phrase.

NOT: The birds built a nest; in the gutters of the roof.

BUT: The birds built a nest in the gutters of the roof.

To introduce a list or a series.

NOT: The documentary described five kinds of intelligence; analytical, social, physical, verbal, and mathematical.

BUT: The documentary described five kinds of intelligence: analytical, social, physical, verbal, and mathematical.

32

The Colon

Colons are used to introduce statements that recapitulate, summarize, or explain an independent clause. Colons are also used to introduce a list or a quotation.

32a To summarize or amplify material in a sentence

➤ It had been a typical day on the job: he set up his waiter station, served throngs of customers, and cleaned up before heading home, exhausted, at midnight.

(Note that some style guides recommend capitalizing the first word following a colon when it introduces an independent clause. See Chapter 36.)

32b To introduce a list when the words preceding the colon make up an independent clause

➤ These are the requirements for the course: faithful attendance, active participation, and timely submission of assignments.

32c To introduce a quotation

➤ Hemingway's "The Short Life of Francis Macomber" begins with this sentence: "It was lunchtime and they were all sitting under the dining tent pretending that nothing had happened."

32d For the following conventional purposes

To follow the salutation of a letter

➤ Dear Sir:

To indicate hours and minutes

➤ 6:45 p.m.

To show ratios and proportions

➤ 3:1

To separate titles from subtitles

➤ Emily Dickinson: A Critical Introduction

To separate city from publication in works cited list entries

➤ New York: Random House

32e Misuses of the colon

Avoid using a colon in the following situations:

Between a verb and its object or complement.

NOT: We brought: money, clothing, and our plane tickets.

BUT: We brought money, clothing, and our plane tickets.

Between a preposition and its object.

NOT: The program consists of: three major parts.

BUT: The program consists of three major parts.

Following the words *including* and *such as*.

NOT: *The Scribner Essentials* explains how to use punctuation marks such as: the semicolon and the colon

BUT: *The Scribner Essentials* explains how to use punctuation marks such as the semicolon and the colon.

33

The Apostrophe

The apostrophe's (') primary use is to indicate possession or ownership.

33a To form the possessive case of nouns and indefinite pronouns

➤ Georgia O'Keeffe's paintings of flowers are among her most beautiful.

➤ It was really nobody's fault.

For singular proper nouns ending in *-'s*, most writers add *-'s* to show possession, but some add only an apostrophe: *Yeats's* poems; *Yeats'* poems.

For singular common nouns ending in *-'s*, add an apostrophe and an *s: boss's, class's.*

33b To indicate the possessive case of plural nouns by adding the apostrophe and *-s* for words not ending in *-s*

➤ The *children's* books of E. B. White have become classics of our literature.

➤ The *women's* movement was launched by Friedan's *The Feminine Mystique*.

For plural nouns ending in *-s*, add only the apostrophe: *Girls'* clothing is on this floor.

33c To indicate the possessive case of compound words and phrases add apostrophe and *-s* to the last word

➤ My *father-in-law's* trips to Italy, France, and Spain have provided him with some of his most memorable dining experiences.

➤ It was *nobody else's* affair.

33d To show joint possession, add an apostrophe and -s to the last noun when two or more nouns are joined by *and*.

➤ *David and Hilda's* new condominium is tastefully furnished.

33e To take the place of missing letters in a contraction (a word with a missing letter)

➤ *Let's* all begin together. (Let us all begin together.)

➤ We *don't* need this much food. (We do not need this much food.)

33f To pluralize letters mentioned as letters

➤ Three large *A*'s adorned his papers.

33g Misuses of the apostrophe

Do not use the apostrophe in the following situations:

To form the possessives of personal pronouns and adjectives.

NOT: his' hers' its' whose'

BUT: his hers its whose

With nouns that are not possessives.

NOT: Most contestants' were very well prepared for the game.

BUT: Most contestants were very well prepared for the game.

To pluralize abbreviations or numbers.

NOT: ID's GRE's in the 1500's.

BUT: IDs GREs in the 1500s.

34

Quotation Marks

Quotation marks, used in pairs (" ") at the beginning and end of a quotation and used singly (' ') in quotes within quotes, tell your readers that certain words have been borrowed from a source.

34a To enclose direct quotations

➤ Abraham Lincoln said that "a house divided against itself cannot stand."

Exception: When a long quotation has been set off from the text in a research paper by indenting, quotation marks are unnecessary.

Use single quotation marks to enclose a quotation within a quotation.

➤ In one of his essays, Russell Baker remarks, "I know what 'the price has been adjusted' means in New Age Babble. It means 'the price is going up.' "

34b To enclose titles of poems, stories, essays, articles, and definitions

➤ Three business magazines ran articles entitled "The Mommy Track."

➤ The Italian words *la dolce vita* can be translated "the sweet life."

34c To set off words as words

➤ The words "imply" and "infer" are frequently confused.

34d Misuses of quotation marks

Do not use quotation marks to highlight slang words, clichés, or for humor.

NOT: Theirs was not the most "exciting" of relationships.

BUT: Theirs was not the most exciting of relationships.

NOT: Every October I travel to Vermont to see the "totally awesome" foliage.

BUT: Every October I travel to Vermont to see the totally awesome foliage.

34e Conventions for using quotation marks with other punctuation

You will often need to use quotation marks with other punctuation marks. The following guidelines explain how to use quotation marks with periods, commas, semicolons, colons, question marks, exclamation points, and dashes.

Periods and Commas   Periods and commas usually appear immediately before closing quotation marks.

➤ "It was not the first time this happened," she said. "Nor will it be the last."

For sentences that end with a parenthetical citation of a source (e.g., a page number or an author and page number), place the period after the citation.

➤ In his book *The Great War and Modern Memory*, Paul Fussell describes the German trenches as "efficient, clean, pedantic, and permanent" (45).

Semicolons and Colons   Semicolons and colons appear immediately after closing quotation marks.

➤ Some thought it necessary to engage in what George Orwell describes as "doublespeak"; most, however, saw no reason for it.

➤ George Orwell coined the term "doublespeak": language used hypocritically to give a false impression, usually an opposite impression of what is true.

Usage Note   Unlike American conventions, British publications place colons and semicolons before the closing quotation marks rather than after.

Question Marks, Exclamation Points, and Dashes   If a question mark, exclamation point, or dash is part of the quotation, place it before closing quotation marks. If a mark of punctuation is not part of the quotation, place it after closing quotation marks.

PART OF QUOTATION

➤ "Did you call?" he asked.

➤ "Leave him alone!" we shouted.

➤ "If you do, I'll—" she warned.

NOT PART OF QUOTATION

➤ Do you remember the story "The Most Dangerous Game"?

➤ I loved the *Seinfeld* episode "The Raincoat"!

➤ "Get with it"—that's an expression I just can't stand.

35

Other Punctuation Marks

The period, question mark, and exclamation point indicate where one sentence ends and another begins. All three marks are thus considered **end punctuation** (or terminal punctuation) marks. More often than not you will punctuate the end of a sentence with a period, but you have some choice between using a period, a question mark, or an exclamation point.

35a The period

Use a period (.) to end a sentence that makes a statement or gives a mild command.

STATEMENTS: The day was unlike any she had ever experienced.

These are the times that try our souls.

MILD COMMANDS: Let your imagination soar.

Give me my arrows of desire.

Use a period for an indirect question, which implies a question rather than asks it directly.

INDIRECT QUESTION: I have often wondered why some people learn languages easily.

INDIRECT QUESTION: Students often ask what it takes to earn an *A*.

Most abbreviations take periods. Note, however, that the abbreviations in the last two columns of the following list may be written with or without periods. Whichever style you adopt, make sure you use it consistently. If you are not sure how to punctuate an abbreviation, look it up in your dictionary.

Mr.	i.e.	B.A. (or BA)	A.D. (or AD)
Mrs.	e.g.	M.A. (or MA)	B.C.E. (or BCE)
Ms.	etc.	Ph.D. (or PhD)	U.S.S.R. (or USSR)
Rev.	a.m.	M.D. (or MD)	U.K. (or UK)
Dr.	p.m.	J.D. (or JD)	U.S.A. (or USA)

Do not include periods when using the postal abbreviations for states.

FL   TN   CA

However, you can write either Washington, DC, or Washington, D.C.

Do not use a period when abbreviating names of organizations, companies, and agencies: *NAACP* (National Association for the Advancement of Colored People), *EPA* (Environmental Protection Agency), *CNN* (Cable News Network). **Acronyms**—abbreviations that are also pronounced as words—omit the period: *AIDS* (acquired immune deficiency syndrome), *NASA* (National Aeronautics and Space Administration), *NOW* (National Organization for Women).

35b The question mark

The question mark (?) is used most often after direct questions. Direct questions often begin with an interrogative word (*who, what, when, why, how*); they usually involve inverted word order.

➤ When is the question mark used?

➤ Where have all the flowers gone?

➤ It is drizzling, is it not?

➤ Do you understand this rule?

Indirect questions are followed by a period rather than a question mark: *I often wondered when a question mark should be used.* The word order in an indirect quotation is not inverted.

➤ We never did find out where all the flowers went.

Writing Hint   You may use question marks within sentences to indicate questions in a series.

➤ I had trouble resolving a number of questions: who would come on the trip? what would our itinerary be? how long would we remain abroad?

You can also punctuate such questions as complete independent sentences.

➤ I had trouble resolving a number of questions. Who would come on the trip? What would our itinerary be? How long would we remain abroad?

Both methods are grammatically correct. Notice, however, that the single-sentence version creates a more swiftly moving sentence. Using capital letters to begin new sentences slows down the pace. Use the method that best serves your rhetorical purpose.

The question mark can also be used to express uncertainty about a date, number, or word.

➤ Geoffrey Chaucer, 1343(?)–1400, author of the *Canterbury Tales*, held a number of court appointments, including collector of taxes.

Do not use a question mark to indicate uncertainty about an event.

INCORRECT: It will snow (?) over the weekend.

CORRECT: It might snow over the weekend.

35c   The exclamation point

Use the exclamation point (!) to indicate surprise or strong emotion. You may also use the exclamation point to give a command.

➤ Help!   ➤ What a gifted comedian she is!

➤ Oh no!   ➤ On your marks! Get set! Go!

Do not use a period or a comma after an exclamation point in direct quotation.

FAULTY: He exclaimed, "I can't believe what I'm hearing!".

REVISED: He exclaimed, "I can't believe what I'm hearing!"

Exclamations are more likely to occur in speech, where we can use our voices to indicate the emotion. They usually do not work as well in writing. Use exclamation points sparingly in academic writing, for they can be distracting. They also tend to exaggerate the importance of a point by calling too much attention to it. (Exclamation points shout!) Overreliance on the exclamation point results, ironically, in a lack of emphasis.

35d   The dash

The dash—used singly or in pairs—interrupts a sentence to insert information, sometimes emphatically.

Use dashes to insert illustrative, explanatory, or emphatic comments.

> I remember a day in class when he leaned far forward in his characteristic pose—the pose of a man about to impart a secret—and croaked, "If you don't know how to pronounce a word, say it loud!"
>
> —E. B. White, "Will Strunk"

> It is a serious matter to shoot a working elephant—it is comparable to destroying a huge and costly piece of machinery—and obviously one ought not to do it if it can possibly be avoided.
>
> —George Orwell, "Shooting an Elephant"

Use dashes to indicate a shift in tone, a hesitation in speech, or a break in thought

> The engaged girls—how many of them there seem to be!—flash their rings and tangle their ankles in their long New Look skirts.
>
> —Cynthia Ozick, "Washington Square, 1956"

Use dashes to introduce or comment on a list

➤ Honesty, decency, integrity, generosity—these were the ideals by which she determined to live.

35e Parentheses

Use parentheses to enclose words, phrases, and clauses of secondary importance to a sentence.

➤ The author's first novel (written on a summer fishing trip in Vermont) is almost entirely autobiographical.

Use parentheses to enclose numbers and letters within lists.

➤ We can isolate four major areas for investigation: (1) social; (2) political; (3) economic; (4) environmental.

35f Brackets

Use brackets to enclose parenthetical elements already within parentheses.

➤ The overwhelming concern (at least according to EPA [Environmental Protection Agency] officials) was that the oil spill be contained.

Use brackets to enclose words inserted into quotations.

➤ According to Ortega, "[Suarez] possessed [charisma] to an extraordinary degree."

35g The slash

Use the slash to indicate line divisions in poetry quoted within a text, to separate terms, and to separate parts of short-hand dates.

➤ The last lines of the poem convey the speaker's sense of regret: "What did I know, what did I know / Of love's austere and lonely offices?"

➤ She took the course with a pass/fail option.

➤ 5/27/99

35h The ellipsis mark

Use ellipses (. . .) to indicate a pause or hesitation.

➤ What I'm looking for is . . . another opportunity to cash in on stock market mania.

➤ And the winner of this year's award for best picture is . . . *Shakespeare in Love.*

Use ellipses enclosed within brackets to indicate omitted material.

Omission of Words in the Middle of a Sentence

➤ "Literacy," writes James Boyd white, "is [. . .] the ability to participate fully in a set of social and intellectual practices."

Be sure to put a space between the second and third ellipsis dots, and add a space before and after the brackets—as shown in the example.

Omission of Words from Different Sentences

➤ "Literacy," writes James Boyd White, "is [. . .] the ability to participate fully in a set of social and intellectual practices. [. . .] It is [. . .] active [. . .] creative [. . .] participation in the speaking and writing of language."

Notice the period before the second ellipsis. This period is not part of the ellipsis, which is enclosed in brackets. Instead, the period represents the end of a sentence.

Omission of Words at the End of a Sentence

➤ James Boyd White writes, "Literacy is not merely the capacity to understand the conceptual content of writings and utterances [. . .]."

Whenever ellipsis marks occur after a gramatically complete sentence, include this fourth dot without any space before it—as shown in the example. Note also that the closing quotation marks come after the end punctuation.

But if your quotation includes a parenthetical reference to a source, place the end punctuation after the parenthetical source citation. In this case, follow the closing brackets immediately with the closing quotation mark, a space, the parenthetical reference, and the sentence period—as in the following example.

➤ James Boyd White writes, "Literacy is not merely the capacity to understand the conceptual content of writings and utterances [. . .]" (23).

36
Capitals

A good college dictionary provides guidance in using capitals. Here are a few important guidelines for using them.

36a Capitalize the first word of a sentence

Always capitalize the first word of a sentence.

➤ This is the most rigorous course I have ever taken. Can you help me?

A number of capitalizing situations require the writer to choose a particular style and then stick with it.

Capitals with Sentences Following Colons When using colons you may or may not use capitals for the first letter that follows the colon. Be consistent with the style you choose.

➤ She welcomed the opportunity to perform: It meant a lot to her.

➤ She welcomed the opportunity to perform: it meant a lot to her.

36b Capitalize the first word of a quotation

When using quotations, capitalize the first word of full-sentence quotations, except when the quote is introduced by the word "that."

➤ The motto "Live free or die" appears on New Hampshire license plates.

➤ Is it true that "it's better to be a live dog than a dead lion"?

Interrupted Quotations When you break up a sentence from a quotation with words of your own, do not capitalize the word that begins the second part of the quotation sentence. Capitalize the first part if it is capitalized in the original.

ORIGINAL QUOTATION
➤ "I have nothing to declare but my genius."

INTERRUPTED QUOTATION
➤ "I have nothing to declare," Oscar Wilde told U.S. custom officials, "but my genius."

36c Capitalize proper nouns and adjectives

Use capitals for **proper nouns** (names of specific people, places, and things): *Lisette, Paris,* the *Eiffel Tower.* Use capitals for **proper adjectives** (adjectives formed from proper nouns): a *Parisian* cafe. Do not capitalize articles (*a, an, the*) accompanying proper nouns or proper adjectives.

When proper nouns are used in a common or everyday context, they are not capitalized.

➤ Please *xerox* the report.

When you use a common noun as an integral part of a proper name—*college*, for example, as in *Boston College*—capitalize the common noun. Words such as *street, river, county, prize*, and *award* are capitalized only when they become part of a specific (proper) term: *Basin Street*, the *Mississippi River, Dade County, Pulitzer Prize, Academy Award*.

36d Capitalize titles of individuals

Capitalize titles when used before a proper name. Do not capitalize titles that follow a proper name or titles used alone.

➤ Justice Scalia   Antonin Scalia, a Supreme Court justice

➤ Governor Christine Todd Whitman   Christine Todd Whitman, governor of New Jersey

➤ Professor Howard Livingston   Howard Livingston, an English professor

➤ Doctor Maria Velásquez   Maria Velásquez, a local doctor

36e Capitalize academic institutions and courses

Capitalize the names of specific schools, departments, and courses. Do not capitalize common nouns for institutions or areas of study.

➤ University of Michigan   a Michigan university
➤ Economics Department   an economics major
➤ Biology 101   an introductory biology course

Writing Hint When referring to words in foreign languages such as Italian, French, or Spanish, be careful to respect its rules of capitalization, which may differ from those in English. For example, the names of the seasons and the days of the week, which begin with capital letters in English, begin with lowercase letters in many other languages, including those named above.

37

Abbreviations

Abbreviations serve as a form of shorthand. They enable writers to replace long names and titles with simple, brief sets of letters. A convenience, abbreviations can help writing and reading become more efficient.

37a Abbreviate personal and professional titles and academic degrees

Some personal and professional titles and some academic degrees are abbreviated when placed before or after a name.

➤ Mr. Magnus Larsen ➤ Mrs. Bizet

➤ Ms. Anne Fujiyoshi ➤ Dr. Weber *or* Kaare Weber, M.D.

➤ Robert M. Chang, Jr. ➤ Archangelo Narazitti, LL.D.

37b Use the abbreviations *a.m., p.m., B.C. (BC), A.D. (AD),* and symbols

Using *a.m.* and *p.m.* The abbreviations *a.m.* and *p.m.* should be used only with exact times.

➤ Class begins at *11:15 a.m.* and ends at *1:15 p.m.*, exactly two hours later.

The notation *a.m.* abbreviates the Latin *ante meridiem*, meaning "before noon"; *p.m.* abbreviates the Latin *post meridiem*, meaning "after noon."

Usage Note The abbreviations *a.m.* and *p.m.* should be used only with numbers, never with the words *morning, evening,* and *night.*

INCORRECT: We met at 7:30 p.m. in the evening.

REVISED: We met at 7:30 p.m.

REVISED: We met at seven-thirty in the evening.

Using *B.C. (BC)* and *A.D. (AD)* In abbreviations for years, place *B.C.* ("before Christ") or *B.C.E.* (before the common era") after the year: *500 B.C.; 5000 B.C.E.* Place *A.D.* (*anno Domini*—"the year of the Lord") or *C.E.* ("common era") before the year: *A.D. 1066; C.E. 1995.* Note that you should use these abbreviations only when your readers may be confused about the time period you are referring to: *The Hopewell culture flourished in what is now the Midwest of the United States from 100 B.C. to A.D. 550.*

37c Use Latin abbreviations for documentation

In general, avoid using the following Latin abbreviations except when citing sources in a research paper or when making a parenthetical point.

Abbreviation	Meaning
i.e.	that is (*id est*)
e.g.	for example (*exempli gratia*)
etc.	and so forth (*et cetera*)
cf.	compare (*confer*)
et al.	and others (*et alia*)
N.B.	note well (*nota bene*)

INAPPROPRIATE: Some companies provide extensive benefits for their employees; e.g., they offer health and dental plans, vacation time, stock options, etc.

REVISED: Some companies provide extensive benefits for their employees; for example, they offer health and dental plans, vacation time, stock options, and the like.

> **Writing Hint** Avoid ending a sentence with an abbreviation. A sentence that ends with *etc.*, for example, gives readers the impression that you ran out of examples or did not bother to provide specifics.

38
Numbers

38a Spell out numbers of one or two words

In a nontechnical piece of writing that uses numbers, if you can spell out a number in one or two words, do so.

➤ The twenty-five members of the class were all present for the party.

When a sentence contains some numbers that should be spelled out and others that should be written as figures, make sure to use one convention consistently.

INCONSISTENT: Our cruise was a short one hundred miles; other vacationers elected longer trips—up to 475 miles.

CONSISTENT: Our cruise was a short 100 miles; other vacationers elected longer trips—up to 475 miles.

38b Spell out numbers at the beginning of a sentence

Always spell out numbers that begin a sentence. However, sentences that begin with spelled-out numbers of more than two words can be awkward and difficult to read. In that case, revise the sentence to begin with another word.

INCORRECT: 100,000 or more marchers demonstrated at the rally.

REVISED: More than 100,000 marchers demonstrated at the rally.

AWKWARD: One hundred fifty-seven million dollars was the selling price of the two companies combined.

REVISED: The selling price of the two companies combined was $157 million.

Writing Hint When you use more than one number to modify a noun, spell out the first number or the shorter of the two numbers to avoid confusion: *six 8-inch slats, 300 one-gallon containers.*

39
Italics

39a Use italics for titles

Use italics to indicate the titles of long or complete works such as novels. Titles of shorter works, such as poems and essays, and titles of sections of works, such as chapters, are set off with quotation marks.

39b Use italics for words, letters, numbers, and phrases used as words

➤ The word *groovy* has dropped out of current usage.

➤ The letter *y* is not part of the Italian alphabet.

Titles to Italicize (or Underline)

BOOKS
Pride and Prejudice

FILMS
Casablanca

PLAYS
A Doll House

LONG POEMS
The Prelude

NEWSPAPERS
the *Atlanta Constitution*

MAGAZINES
Newsweek

PAMPHLETS
Dangerous Drugs

WORKS OF VISUAL ART
van Gogh's *Starry Night*

MUSICAL WORKS
Tchaikovsky's *Nutcracker*

TELEVISION AND RADIO PROGRAMS
Prime Time Live

RECORDINGS
Bruce Springsteen's *Born to Run*

JOURNALS
Nursing Review

PUBLISHED SPEECHES
Lincoln's *Gettysburg Address*

EXCEPTIONS
Titles of sacred works and their parts as well as public documents do not take italics.

the Bible
the New Testament
the Koran

the Bill of Rights
the U.S. Constitution
the Magna Carta

> Robert Parish wore the number *00* when he played for the Boston Celtics.

> Who coined the phrase *over the hill*?

39c   Use italics for foreign words and phrases

English has acquired many words from foreign languages. Many of these words are now part of the English language and should not be italicized: spaghetti (Italian), chef (French), kindergarten (German), mesa (Spanish). To find out whether a word or expression is considered foreign, look it up in a dictionary.

> The famous opening movement of Beethoven's Fifth Symphony is marked *allegro ma non troppo* (fast, but not too fast).

> The common sunflower, *Helianthus annuus*, has a tall coarse stem and large, yellow-rayed flower heads that produce edible seeds rich in oil.

39d   Use italics for the names of trains, ships, aircraft, and spacecraft

Although you should italicize the names of specific trains, ships, aircraft, and spacecraft, do not italicize general types and classes of these vehicles.

➤ We took Amtrak's *Empire Builder* to Seattle.

➤ We rode the Metroliner between Boston and Washington.

TRAINS
➤ the *Orient Express*   the *Silver Streak*

SHIPS
➤ the *Nina*   *U.S.S. Constitution*

AIRCRAFT AND SPACECRAFT
➤ the *Spirit of St. Louis*   the space shuttle *Endeavor*

Writing Hint   Be aware of the visual effect of italics when you write. Italic type can be used to highlight key terms or concepts. It can also be used for heads and subheads in longer papers and reports.

40

Hyphens

Hyphenation occurs most often for the simple reason that a word is too long to fit at the end of a line of type. In such cases the writer divides the word, putting part of the word at the end of one line and the remainder of the word at the beginning of the next line. Writers also use hyphens to join words or parts of words, as in *go-between* and *knick-knack*. Do not confuse a **hyphen** (-) with a dash (—), which is made by combining two hyphens.

40a Use hyphens to divide words at the end of a line

Conventions for Dividing Words at the End of a Line

- Do not divide one-syllable words, even long ones such as *thought* and *health*.

- Although the first letter of a word may comprise a syllable, do not leave one letter on a line. Leave at least two letters on each line when dividing a word.

  INCORRECT: Guard against infection by applying an i-
    odine ointment to the wound.

  REVISED: Guard against infection by applying an io-
    dine ointment to the wound.

- Do not divide abbreviations, contractions, or numbers. *U.S.A.*, *couldn't*, and *50,000* should not be hyphenated.

- Do not hyphenate names of people and places. Neither *Thomas Jefferson* nor his home, *Monticello*, can be hyphenated.

- Only divide words between syllables. You cannot hyphenate the word *recess*, for example, as *rec-ess* but only as *re-cess*.

- Divide compound words only between the words that form the compound. Split the word *homecoming*, for example, across two lines as *home-coming*, not as *ho-mecoming* or *homecom-ing*.

- Divide words according to their prefixes and suffixes. Divide *subordinate* after the prefix (*sub-ordinate*) and the word *fairly* before the suffix (*fair-ly*).

- Remember to attach the hyphen to the part of the word on the first line and not to the part of the word that begins the next line.

40b Use hyphens with compound words

Compound words consist of two or more words joined together as a single word. Some are written as one word, others as hyphenated words, and still others as separate words without hyphens.

ONE WORD: skyline, scarecrow, outlaw

HYPHENATED: brother-in-law, cross-examination, nation-state

SEPARATE: junior high, energy guide, ice cream

Hyphens with Compound Adjectives Use a hyphen for **compound adjectives.**

➤ Venus Williams is a world-renowned tennis star.

Do not use a hyphen when part of the compound adjective ends in *-ly*.

➤ The surprisingly short concert disappointed the audience.

Hyphens with Coined Compounds A **coined compound** connects words not ordinarily linked or hyphenated. Use coined compounds sparingly in formal and academic writing; reserve them to create an informal tone.

➤ They were in a let-it-all-hang-out frame of mind.

Hyphens with Fractions and Compound Numbers Use a hyphen when spelling out fractions to connect the numerator and denominator.

➤ The cake was one-quarter finished before dinner even began.

➤ The strip of wood was three-eighths of an inch wide.

Also use a hyphen to spell out whole numbers from twenty-one through ninety-nine, even when those numbers are part of larger numbers.

➤ one thousand thirty-five

➤ eighty thousand six hundred fifty-two

Usually compound numbers are expressed as figures.

Hyphens in a Series   Use a hyphen for a series of compound words built on the same base. Be sure to leave a space after the first word.

➤ First- and second-generation immigrants composed the class.

Writing Hint   It is sometimes difficult to determine when to hyphenate a compound word. Conventions shift rapidly and are unpredictable. Even compound words that begin with the same word are treated differently: *breakthrough*, *break dance*, *break-in*. And although many words pass through successive stages—from two words (*base ball*) to a hyphenated form (*base-ball*) to a single word (*baseball*)—some remain at the first or second stage. Consult your dictionary for help with hyphenating compound words.

40c   Use hyphens with prefixes and suffixes

Prefixes are generally combined with word stems without hyphens: *pre*fatory, *inter*view, *dis*belief, *non*compliant, *re*elect. In cases where the prefix precedes a capital letter or when a capital letter is combined with a word, separate the two with a hyphen: anti-American, pre-Columbian, H-bomb.

Certain prefixes, such as *all-*, *self-*, *quasi-*, and *ex-* (to mean "formerly"), normally take a hyphen when combined with words: *all*-encompassing, *self*-denial, *ex*-player, *quasi*-convincing.

Very few suffixes take a hyphen. Two of these are *-elect* and *-some*, as in governor-*elect* and twenty-*some*.

Writing Hint   Do not capitalize words containing the prefix *ex-* and the suffix *-elect*, even in titles with proper names.

INCORRECT: Ex-Mayor Bradley

REVISED: ex-Mayor Bradley

INCORRECT: Governor-Elect Ramirez

REVISED: Governor-elect Ramirez

part 7

Writing for Special Purposes

41
Business Writing

In writing for business and the professions follow the basic principles presented below.

- **Know your audience.** Be aware of who will receive and read what you write. Try to use his or her name—at the very least you should know the individual's title and level of authority. Avoid outdated forms of address such as *Dear Sir.*
- **Express your purpose.** Explain quickly and clearly your reason for writing.
- **Be polite.** Use a courteous and civilized tone. Be friendly but not overly informal.
- **Be concise.** Say what you have to say as directly and briefly as possible.
- **Be clear.** Make sure your language can be easily understood.
- **Use correct grammar, punctuation, and mechanics.** Take pains to ensure that your writing follows the conventions of standard English. Doing so will indicate your concern for accuracy and your attention to detail.
- **Consider appearances.** Be neat. Use high-quality bond paper. Make your work look pleasing to the eye. If you are working on a word processor, experiment with various formatting options to produce an attractive document.

41a Business memos

Memos serve a number of purposes. Primarily, they maintain open channels of communication within a company—colleagues keep one another apprised of events with informal memos. Memos are also used to call meetings or to announce changes in policy. In addition, memos serve as a permanent record of decisions made and actions undertaken. They may contain information regarding approaches to problems, or they may express attitudes toward company policies.

Memos contain evidence that can be used to enhance or diminish your job performance. Thus, it is a good idea to avoid writing anything ungracious or unkind in your memos. In particular, be careful to avoid biased language. In writing memos, keep the accompanying conventions in mind.

- Follow the proper format, identifying the date of the memo, its audience, sender, and subject at the top of the page.

- Single-space long memos; double-space short ones.
- Initial the memo next to your name.
- Keep the memo brief and to the point.
- Engage your readers by focusing on essential matters, one idea per paragraph. Begin with the most important idea.
- Conclude with a gesture of goodwill.

41b Business letters

Business letters serve as a company's primary means of external communication. A business letter is also the appropriate form of communication for an individual writing to a company. Whether you are writing to seek information, place an order, request an adjustment, lodge a complaint, or attend to some other business matter, you should follow the principles of business communication listed on page 144.

You should also use one of the standard formats for business letters: block or modified block. *Block format* aligns everything at the left margin. *Modified block* format uses indents. Whichever format you use, be sure to observe the conventions of spacing consistently.

41c Correspondence as e-mail

Follow the same guidelines for business letters you send by e-mail as for those you send via conventional mail. Express your purpose clearly, write succinctly and grammatically, and maintain a courteous and professional tone. Since e-mail letters tend to be less formal than traditionally printed ones, you may adopt a slightly less formal style, but be careful to avoid colloquialisms and an overly breezy casual style.

The following steps will help you write effective e-mail for business correspondence.

- Identify your main topic in the subject line.
- Provide necessary context and background in your opening sentence.
- Clarify your purpose quickly.
- Zero in on the main point early.
- Try to keep your message to a single screen.

41d Résumés

A *résumé* is a succinct outline of your educational background and work experience, coupled with information about your related extracurricular activities and special skills or

SAMPLE BUSINESS LETTER IN BLOCK FORMAT

return address	1234 Gray Street Glen Ellyn, IL 54321
date line space	April 25, 1999
inside address	Ms. Angela Hernandez Publicity Department Cannon Electric Company 35 Harvest Drive Chicago, IL 35791
line space salutation line space	Dear Ms. Hernandez:

I am writing to request information about your company's products and services for a research paper I am preparing for my marketing course at Northwestern University. The instructor suggested that in addition to the usual library research, we could gain a different perspective by reading publications produced by various companies. Hence my request.

line space

I am a senior marketing major with a special interest in electrical products and services. I am particularly interested in research and development your company may be engaged in as well as in your company's relationship with suppliers and clients.

line space

I appreciate your taking the time to send me any company publications you think suitable. And if there were the slightest chance you would have time to speak with me in person, I would be happy to come to Cannon Electric at a time convenient for you.

line space
closing   Sincerely yours,
4 line spaces

signature   *Boris Rodzinski*

name, typed   Boris Rodzinski

                 c. Professor K. Evancie

interests. Résumés may be arranged according to your specific job skills (a functional résumé) or according to the jobs you have held, beginning with the most recent (a chronological résumé). Functional résumés are suitable when you have acquired significant work experience, well-developed skills, and significant accomplishments. Chronological résumés are more common for someone entering the marketplace for the first time or for those with only modest work experience. Use the accompanying guidelines in preparing your résumé.

- Place your name, address, and phone number at the top of the page.
- Include clearly labeled categories for career objective, education, work experience, special skills, activities, and references.
- Include dates for graduation and for time at each job.
- If you are preparing a chronological résumé, place educational and work experience in reverse chronological order, beginning with the most recent job.
- Provide a brief description of your responsibilities at each job.
- Include a title for each job or position held.
- Try to keep the résumé to a single page so it can be scanned quickly.
- Use a uniform type size for headings, a different type size for information beneath the headings. If you are working on a word processor, take advantage of the available lettering and formatting options.
- Space your categories evenly and make your résumé as pleasing to the eye as you can. Leave ample space between entries, avoid crowding, and be sure the résumé is perfect in appearance.

Preparing a Scannable Résumé There are some important differences between traditional and scannable résumés. Because computer scanning of résumés capitalizes on key word searches, and since key words tend to be nouns rather than verbs or adjectives, a scannable résumé needs to be noun-heavy rather than verb-heavy. In a traditional résumé you would emphasize what you accomplished with verbs such as "produced," "maintained," or "developed." In a scannable résumé you should shift to nouns and noun phrases such as "product manager," "maintenance control," or "software developer." In addition, you should create a category for your key word descriptors and place it early to allow for quick identification of your key abilities.

Because computer scanners vary in their ability to distinguish letters and other kinds of symbols on paper, you should make your paper résumé as easy to read and scan as possible.

```
Martha T. Kilmer
North Hall
Pace University
Pleasantville, 10570
914-555-3286

KEY WORDS: Bilingual teacher, Spanish/English
teacher, research experience, youth coordinator,
counselor, public service, community action,
psychology major.

OBJECTIVE: Teaching position with Spanish/English
language skills.

EDUCATION: Bachelor of Arts, Pace University,
May 2001
Major: Psychology (Honors Program)
New York State Teaching Certificate, Grades 7-12.

EXPERIENCE: Research Assistant, Psychology
Department, Pace University, June 1999-March
2000. Recruiter for a computerized study of
mental imagery in adults, children, and
teenagers. Processor of data and statistical
information for the study.

Youth Coordinator, Rindge Teen Shelter, Department
of Human Services, Mt. Kisco, NY, September
1998-May 1999. Counselor and mentor to drop-in
teenagers at the youth shelter. Workshop leader
on adolescent concerns and issues.

SKILLS: Bilingual in Spanish and English.

ACTIVITIES: Coordinator for Neighborhood Develop-
ment Program, a public service and community
action program.

REFERENCES: Available from the Pace University
Career Services Offices, Pleasantville, NY 10570.
```

Preparing an Internet Résumé   You may also wish to post a résumé on the Web, where your résumé is a hyperlink on your home page. Like scannable résumés, Web-based résumés differ from traditional ones. Try to take advantage of the way the Web works by keeping your résumé brief and viewable without scrolling and by including more detail through links. Use the following guidelines to create your Web-based résumé.

- Follow the guidelines for designing a Web site (see Chapter 43).
- Provide links to enhance your résumé with examples of your work, or with more detailed explanations of your accomplishments.
- Put essential information on one easily viewable page.
- Place the most important information—contact data, education, and work experience—in the topmost 300 pixels.
- Include relevant graphics—your photograph—and relevant artwork and images via links to scanned photos or images.
- Provide a practical title for users to easily identify the pages as your résumé.
- Keep your résumé current, and include the most recent date you revise your résumé.

42
Document Design

Graphics convey meaning to readers in the same way as the words of your documents. At their best, graphics complement the information you convey through words. Strive for a balance between text and graphics, always considering how graphics can clarify and accentuate what you say through words. Consider the following guidelines for using graphics.

- Use a flowchart, table, or outline to preview or review.
- Use a chart, diagram, or map to orient readers.
- Use a flowchart or diagram to illustrate sequential or hierarchical relationships.
- Use a bar graph, pie chart, or simple table to emphasize key relationships.
- Use a complex graph, table, or diagram to analyze or summarize data.
- Use a facsimile of a source to illustrate originals.
- Use a photo, cartoon, or other image to arouse interest.

42a General design considerations

Titles   Center titles and print them in the same size and font of type as the essay or paper, or in a larger or bolder typeface.

Headings   Break the text into chunks, with strategically placed headings. By glancing at your headings, readers can gain a quick overview of the specific content elements you have included.

Block Quotations   Set off quotations of more than four lines of prose and three lines of poetry visually as a *block*. This visual separation indicates that you are quoting more than a few words or sentences.

Graphs and Charts   Add graphs and charts to your papers and reports. Such visual aids display information efficiently in far less space and they introduce variety into your papers and reports.

42b Designing documents for academic contexts

Pagination   Number the pages of your document, omitting a page number from the title page. Begin numbering the first page of text consecutively with arabic numerals, usually in the upper right corner.

Margins and Spacing   Type and double-space your academic papers. Indent paragraphs one-half inch, or five spaces. In some circumstances, such as preparing science lab reports or reports for business courses, you may use single-spacing.

Justify, or align, the lines of print to the left margin of your writing. Indent for new paragraphs and for lists and block quotations. In academic papers, however, it is common to leave the right margin *unjustified*, or ragged.

Type Size and Style   Use a common easy-to-read 10- or 11-point size in a simple font. Stick with a single font and type size for your academic papers and reports—except for headings and titles, as explained earlier.

Highlighting   You may occasionally highlight words with italics, boldface, or capital letters. Use these features only for headings and titles.

Headings   Use headings to announce the focus of sections within your writing. For longer reports and research papers, however, headings can help focus readers' attention on particular aspects of your topic.

Lists Bulleted lists allow you to isolate and emphasize key points. They can also enhance the visual appeal of a document. In using bulleted lists, however, be careful not to make them too long. Lists of more than ten items should be grouped into two categories. Also, keep the items in the list to a single line each. And be sure that the items are grammatically parallel. In some instances, you may wish to number the items rather than bullet them.

White Space The space around the print on a page acts like a frame for a picture. It focuses the reader's attention on the printed text; it also creates a contrast between the dark print and the complementary white background against which that print stands out. For most academic writing, frame your pages with margins of 1 to 1½ inches all around, depending on the audience, purpose, and content of your document.

In preparing visuals, strive for a clean appearance, with plenty of white space around them. Visuals should complement your written text, add to it, or summarize information efficiently.

Pie Chart This *pie chart* illustrates how state lottery proceeds for a thirty-year period 1964–1995 were allocated. Although the information could be presented in alternative formats such as a list, table, or bar graph, the pie chart lets readers see the relative weight in percentages for each area of allocation. In general, use pie charts to portray relationships among parts and a whole.

Percent distribution of 1964–1995
cumulative State lottery proceeds
($93 billion)

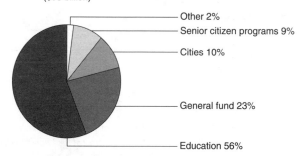

Other 2%
Senior citizen programs 9%
Cities 10%
General fund 23%
Education 56%

Sample Pie Chart

Line Graph The sample *line graph* represents media usage by consumers for a ten-year period. Each line represents a different type of media. The direction of each line indicates an increase or decrease in the use of particular media. Use line graphs to display trends and multiple line graphs to compare trends over time.

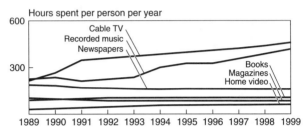

Media Usage by Consumers: 1989 to 1999

Sample Line Graph

Bar Graph The sample *bar graph* describes software sales for 1994 and 1995 in millions of dollars. Different types of software programs are included with the most used on top and the less used on the bottom. Use bar graphs to display comparative information visually.

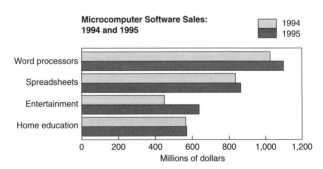

Sample Bar Graph

All charts adapted from the U.S. Bureau of the Census. From *The American Almanac 1996–1997 Statistical Abstract of the United States*, Hoover's, Inc., Austin Texas, 1997, 296, 558.

Guidelines for Using Visuals

- Provide a caption or legend for each visual.
- Make sure the details of your visuals are clear and readable.
- Number your visuals.
- Provide a lead-in comment in your written text to introduce each visual.
- For complex visuals that contain multiple kinds of information, explain what the visual illustrates.
- Credit the source for visuals you do not create yourself.

43

Writing and Designing for the World Wide Web

43a Composing Web pages

If you've done much Web surfing, you know that there are a lot of very poor pages on the Internet: pages with silly dancing gophers, hideous colors, and unreadable text; pages that make you wonder why someone bothered to publish them, and pages that take forever to load onto your computer. With more and more people publishing Web pages, clear standards for effective, tasteful pages are being developed.

43b Characteristics of good Web pages

In general, your pages should meet the following criteria:

- **Content.** Be sure you have a reason to create the page. Composing a Web page is *real writing*: millions of people may see your page. Don't waste their time. The rule is "value-added"—if you are not adding anything of value to the Web, do not add anything at all. A page of nothing but links to other Web pages or pictures of your cat is best left off the Web. Add original content, something that may be useful and interesting for other Web users.
- **Graphics.** On the Web, the visual often rivals the textual in importance, and the two working together create effects that could not be achieved by either one individually. Use

graphics sparingly but effectively. In most cases, images that move, flash, beep, or buzz simply annoy your viewers, even if they seem clever at the time you create the page. And most viewers, research shows, will not wait more than ten or fifteen seconds for huge graphics to show up on their screens.

- **Ease of Navigation.** Moving around your Web site must be easy and intuitive. Make sure your viewers know how to find something on your site and how to get back to where they started. Avoid dead-end pages, which have no links on them for your viewer to move to. Use a table of contents and make it easy for your viewers to get to it from anywhere in your site.

- **Scannability.** Make your pages easy to scan. A viewer should be able to judge the content and value of your page almost instantly, simply by scanning it. Use headings and lists; write short sentences and paragraphs. Highlight your major points visually.

- **Personality.** Give your viewers a sense of who you are. Your page should reflect your tastes, values, and viewpoints. It should also establish you as a credible source of information and knowledge. Viewers of your page are likely to want to know what gives you the authority to compose and publish this particular Web page.

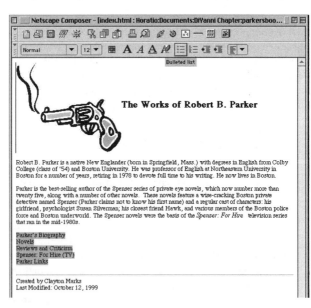

An Effective Web Page

Netscape and the Netscape logo design are all registered trademarks of Netscape Communications Corporation.

Avoid making the following mistakes in your Web pages:

- **Nothing but "Cool Links."** Make sure your page presents some of your own information. While there is some value in collecting your favorite links to other sites and publishing them on the Web for the use of other viewers, your page should be more than a gathering of links. Create your own material; add a short list of appropriate links.
- **Busy Pages.** Avoid pages that have too many distracting colors and images. Although a certain amount of inventiveness and play is natural on the Web, you should avoid novelty for its own sake. Just because you can put an animated picture of singing turtles on your page does not mean you should.
- **Heavy, slow-loading graphics.** Remember that many of your viewers may be working on old computers with slow modems, and graphical material that takes a long time to load will send them running to another page somewhere else on the Web.

43c   Planning and organizing

Basically, composing a Web page is still a form of writing, and you should approach it as you would any writing. To write effectively, you should plan and organize your Web site and each Web page within it. You should collect your materials; then draft and revise your drafts. Finally, carefully edit and proofread your pages.

The first point to remember as you plan your site is to think hypertextually. Hypertext, the underlying concept of the World Wide Web, is the linking together of different pages in a hierarchical organization. The normal reading process of an essay or book is linear: you start at the beginning and read through to the end. In a hypertext document such as a Web site, the viewer has multiple options for where to start and what to read next. The viewer decides what to read and in what order. Thus you cannot count on a viewer starting at the beginning of your Web site and reading straight through to the end. In fact, with the exception of the home page index.html, there is no beginning or end.

Visualize your site as a number of short pages that may be read in any order, the most important of which may be accessed from your site's home page. In this sense, the home page functions as a table of contents, providing an easily scanned overview of your site's topics.

Finding a Subject, Purpose, and Audience   Since composing a Web page and a Web site is simply another form of writing, the techniques you have learned from earlier chapters apply here. If you are assigned a subject for a Web page, you can skip the first step of finding a subject. If not, search your journals, do some brainstorming on paper or in groups, question what you see and hear, or pick a controversy that you have some feelings about. Remember, Web pages grow and evolve just as written compositions do, so you will modify and revise whatever subject you choose anyway. Your initial selection of subject is not binding and should cause no anxiety.

In designing a Web page, purpose is the most important consideration. A page with no purpose should not be published on the Web. Your sense of purpose will evolve as you gather more material, compose, and revise, so you just need a rough sense of purpose to begin your page. Ask yourself what you hope to accomplish with the page, what information you wish to provide, and what interpretation of the information you hope to convey. Decide whether you are trying to convince, persuade, inform.

Your sense of purpose and your sense of audience work closely together. Not only must you arrive at a clear purpose for your Web page, but also you should achieve that purpose with a specific audience in mind. You should not approach a topic in the same way for knowledgeable experts as you do for beginners. Are you trying to inform, convince, or persuade your readers? Who are they? How much do they know? What do they need to know?

Finding External Web Pages to Link to   You almost certainly will want to provide links to other relevant Web sites on your page. As part of your research for your Web page, you should make a running list of Web sites you visit as you research. If you use Internet Explorer to browse the Web, it keeps a record of every site you visit in its "history." If you use Netscape Navigator, you should bookmark every page (or at least every potentially useful page) you visit. Recent versions of both Navigator and Internet Explorer also allow you to annotate your bookmarks (or "favorites"), so you can record brief notes about each site as you visit it.

A variety of good search engines (e.g., Altavista, Hotbot, Northern Light, Infoseek) and Web directories (e.g., Yahoo!) are available to assist your search. Enter your search terms into the search engine and refine your search until you have a workable list of resources. When you find interesting sites, make a note. Keep a list either on your computer (bookmarks/favorites) or in a notebook of Web addresses you visit, along with a brief note describing each site and how it might be useful. Will it be a resource that you include in a list of interesting sites for your viewers to visit? Does it contain information that you will want to link to text you compose for your Web page? Keep refining the list as you research and even as you compose and revise your Web pages.

Finding Graphical Material to Use A huge store of graphical material is available on the Web for your use. Usually any search engine or directory can locate graphics in short order. However, you need to be aware of two issues.

First, it is often difficult to find what you want. If you want simple decorative or thematic clip-art, that is easy to find. If you want a *particular* image—say a picture of Albert Einstein or of the Space Shuttle—that will require a concentrated search. By using the search engines judiciously and refining your queries, you often will be able to find what you need. Some search engines allow your to search a term (say "Einstein") and restrict your results to only images. Or, since all images on the Web must be one of two types—JPEG or GIF—and they must have the file extensions ".jpg" or ".gif," you can add those terms to your query: Einstein AND (.jpg OR .gif).

This brings up the second and perhaps more troublesome issue: copyright violations. Just as with text, every image you find on the Web is automatically copyrighted by its owner. You need to find images that the owner has allowed free use of (there are thousands of free clip-art sites that give blanket permission, although often this permission is restricted to nonprofit sites—read the fine print on the Web site where you get the image). You can also contact the owner of the image and explicitly ask for permission to use the image. Although copyright laws covering the Internet are still evolving and in many respects are chaotic, the best rule to follow is this: if you don't have either blanket or explicit permission to use an image, do not use it.

43d Revising

Revise for Style and Overall Appeal If you have browsed the Web much at all, you know that many Web pages are simply ugly—they lack style, they use clashing and irritating colors and they are confusing to view. Overall, they simply create a bad impression on the viewer. While a complete discussion of the aesthetics of Web page design is beyond the scope of this chapter, here are a few guidelines to help you avoid the most common stylistic mistakes.

1. Limit your graphics both in size (physical size and file size) and number.

2. Make sure they are necessary and appropriate, that they really add something essential to your page.

3. Avoid frivolous and overly cute images that have no relation-ship to the content of the page.

The page should be easily scannable by a viewer, with im-portant points set out in appropriate size headings. Separate ma-jor sections of a page with horizontal rules and relate material chunked together visually on the page. Use lots of white space—create a page that is not dense with long paragraphs of print text. A Web page operates under different conventions from an essay. Do not use a black background; it may feel dar-ing and shocking to you, but almost no text of any color is read-able on a black background.

Finally, consistency is valuable. Keep your colors coordi-nated in pleasing combinations. Use the same size headings for equivalent levels of subpoints on your page. For example, if your page title is in Heading 2, use Heading 3 for all your main points and Heading 4 for all subpoints under each main point. Keep the same system for all pages in your site. This provides a com-fort zone for your viewer, who knows what to expect on each page and how your pages work.

Revise for Content   Revision is probably the most fa-miliar task to you as a writer. As with essays or other papers you may write, your Web pages must have a focus, purpose, and clear conception of the intended audience.

In revising your Web pages, consider all levels of your content: start with the major issues of purpose and focus. Does this page really have a purpose for existing? If so, do you (and your potential viewers) have a clear understanding of what it is, based on the content of the site? Revise your pages until there is nothing extra that will distract and nothing missing that will confuse the viewer. Even though the logic of hypertext is not the logic of the essay or the debating podium, you should try to clear up any illogical jumps of words and ideas on each page. A viewer who cannot follow your thinking will quickly click out of your Web site and go to one that is easier to follow.

Is the writing on the pages clear and concise? Web view-ers tend to be impatient with extra text; cut your writing to its most concise form. Delete extra words; make list-like prose (a a long series of items in sentences) into bulleted lists.

And finally, don't forget the details: grammar, spelling, and punctuation. Even though the Web may seem like the wild west sometimes, the rules of writing must be obeyed. Most Web page composing software, including Netscape Composer, incorporates a spelling checker—use it. Sentence fragments, mistakes in usage, and misspelled words all mark you as an ir-responsible Web site composer and reduce your credibility and authority in the eyes of your viewer.

Glossary of Usage

This glossary provides guidance for using commonly confused words and phrases. The advice offered reflects standard usage for academic and professional writing. It also reflects current opinion among practicing writers on what is considered appropriate for publication. For additional guidance on matters of usage, consult a current dictionary.

a, an Use *a* before words that begin with consonant sounds: *a book*, *a h*istorical argument. Use *an* before words beginning with a vowel sound: *an a*rgument, *an h*onest mistake.

accept, except *Accept* is a verb that means "to receive." She *accepted* his apology. As a preposition, *except* means "to leave out." *Except* for anchovies, he enjoyed all kinds of pizza toppings.

advice, advise *Advice*, a noun, means a "suggestion": Their *advice* was to take a double major. The verb *advise* means "to give advice": I *advise* you to write a letter expressing your appreciation for the special scholarship.

affect, effect The verb *affect* means "to influence" or "move emotionally": Excessive drinking *affected* their judgment. As a verb, *effect* means "to bring about": She wished to *effect* radical change. As a noun, *effect* signifies a result: The *effects* of the war were staggering.

all ready, already *All ready* means "fully prepared"; *already* means "previously" or "before now." We were *all ready* to leave for our trip, having *already* made plane and hotel reservations.

all right, alright Spell *all right* as two words rather than as *alright*.

all together, altogether *All together* means that all are gathered in a group in one place: The committee had never been *all together*. *Altogether* means "entirely": They were *altogether* opposed to the idea.

allusion, illusion An *allusion* is an indirect reference to a person, event, or thing: The *allusion* was to Elvis Presley's habit of gyrating his pelvis in performance. An *illusion* is a deceptive appearance: *Illusions* about the glamor of movie acting draw many to Hollywood.

a lot, alot Spell *a lot* as two words rather than as *alot*. Avoid using the colloquial *a lot* in formal writing to mean "a large amount" or "many."

among, between *Among* indicates relationships among three or more people or things; *between* indicates relationships between two people or things. The proposals were considered *among* the club's four officers; they had to decide *between* retaining their present mission or going in an entirely new direction.

amount, number *Amount* indicates a quantity of something noncountable; *number* refers to things that can be counted. A large *number* of people expended a significant *amount* of effort.

and/or This construction is sometimes used in business or legal writing to indicate that either or both of two things apply: We wanted to buy a new car *and/or* truck. Avoid using *and/or* in formal writing.

anxious, eager *Anxious* means "uneasy or worried": He was *anxious* about his upcoming interview. *Eager* lacks the apprehension of *anxious*, indicating instead "being desirous of something": They were *eager* to begin eating.

anybody, any body; anyone, any one *Anybody* and *anyone* are indefinite pronouns that refer to people but not to particular individuals. Isn't there *anyone* who can tell me how to get to the Brooklyn Bridge? *Any body* and *any one* both refer to specific though unidentified things or individuals: *Any one* of you may begin. Follow the same guidelines for *nobody, no body*, and *no one*.

as Using *as* to substitute for *because* or *since* can result in vagueness or ambiguity. *As* they were preparing for the long journey, they decided to have a hearty breakfast. (It is not clear here whether *as* means *because* or *while*.)

as, like Use *as* to indicate equivalence; use *like* to indicate resemblance. *As* a lecturer, Dr. Benton is outstanding. (Dr. Benton = a lecturer.) *Like* other art historians who offer seasonal lecture series, she has an avid following. (*Like* = similar to.) Use *as* (not *like*) in clauses: You should do *as* I say, not *as* I do.

awful, awfully Avoid *awful* to mean "bad" and *awfully* to mean "very"—at least in formal writing. Literally, if something is *awful* it suggests that it inspires awe or wonder.

awhile, a while *Awhile* means "for a short time"; *a while* means "a time." *Awhile* is an adverb and *while* is a noun: We relaxed *awhile* before studying for *a while* longer.

bad, badly *Bad* is an adjective and *badly* an adverb: They had not been treated *badly*, but they nonetheless felt *bad* about what had happened.

being as, being that Avoid using these expressions in place of *since* or *because*: Because [not *being that*] she completed her work early, she was able to go home.

beside, besides *Beside* is a preposition meaning "next to": Place the chair in the corner *beside* the small table. *Besides*, as an adverb, means "moreover": *Besides*, there is always tomorrow. As a preposition, *besides* means "in addition to": *Besides* an excellent emergency room, the hospital boasts a state-of-the-art neonatal unit.

can, may *Can* indicates an ability to do something; *may* suggests possibility. We *can* learn how to play chess. We *may* even become grand masters. Use *may* rather than *can* to request permission: *May* I go now?

cite, sight, site *Cite* means "to mention" or "to identify a source": In her speech she *cited* a recent article published in the *New England Journal of Medicine*. *Sight* means "to view" (verb) or "a view" (noun): Astronomers recently *sighted* what they believe is a previously undiscovered planet. A *site* is a place or location: This is a perfect *site* to pitch a tent.

complement, compliment *Complement* means "to add to" or "to go well with": Their trip north *complemented* their southern journey of the summer before. *Compliment* means "to praise": He *complimented* her on the outstanding speech she gave as valedictorian.

continual, continuous *Continual* means "repeated at frequent or regular intervals": The *continual* attempts to persuade me to buy were unsuccessful. *Continuous* means "ongoing": The music was *continuous*, never stopping for more than the normal break between songs.

criteria, criterion The words refer to standards of evaluation. *Criterion* is singular; *criteria* is plural. The *criteria* used to evaluate candidates were numerous and diverse.

data It has recently become acceptable to use *data* with a singular verb as well as in the plural: The *data was* gathered under the auspices of the American Council of Churches. The *data were* not clearly supportive of either position.

different from, different than Though the preferred form, *different from* is being joined more and more by *different than* in print as well as in conversation. Their statistics were not very *different from* ours. His statistics were not very *different than* what we had expected.

disinterested, uninterested To be *disinterested* is to be "impartial"; to be *uninterested* means "to be not interested." The judge in the case was *disinterested*. He remained *uninterested* in politics all his life.

due to Use as an adjective following a form of the verb *to be*: The victory *was due to* a persistent and unyielding defense. Avoid using this phrase as a preposition: The committee chair canceled the meeting *because of* (not *due to*) the hurricane.

eager See *anxious, eager.*

effect See *affect, effect.*

elicit, illicit *Elicit* means "to evoke" or "to draw out": The advertisement for subsidized housing *elicited* many applications. *Illicit* means "illegal": The gang had been involved in *illicit* activities for years.

every day, everyday Use *every day* to mean "each day"—an adjective with a noun. Use *everyday* as an adjective that modifies another noun. It was an *everyday* outfit, comfortable and simple—one that could be worn *every day.*

every one, everyone *Everyone* is an indefinite pronoun referring to a group as a whole: *Everyone* participated. *Every one*, an adjective followed by a noun, refers to each member of a group individually: *Every one* of the committee members favored the new plan.

except See *accept, except.*

explicit, implicit *Explicit* means "expressed directly or outright": Her *explicit* instructions were to deposit the money by noon in the savings account. *Implicit* means "implied or suggested": They had an *implicit* understanding between them.

farther, further *Farther* indicates distance only: The museum was *farther* away than I thought. *Further* indicates either distance or degree: When he took office the President attempted to stimulate the economy *further.*

fewer, less Use *fewer* for countable items and *less* for noncountable ones: *Fewer* television programs today portray people smoking than those of a decade ago. There is *less* attention paid to survival skills than there used to be. See also *amount, number.*

good, well *Good* is an adjective: He continued in *good* health *well* into his nineties. *Well* is often an adverb (though it can function as an adjective with verbs denoting a state of being or feeling): He did not feel *well* after eating a *good* two pounds of cole slaw.

hanged, hung The past participle of *hang* is both *hanged* and *hung*. Use *hanged* when referring to executions; use *hung* to mean "suspended." People are *hanged*; pictures are *hung*.

herself, himself, myself, yourself These *-self* pronouns are both reflexive (they refer to an antecedent) and intensive (they intensify an antecedent): I, *myself*, could not go. Do not use these pronouns in place of subjective or objective pronouns: The award went to Barbara and her (not *herself*). No one but you (not *yourself*) can make that decision.

hopefully *Hopefully* means "with hope": The quarterback watched his last pass *hopefully*. Avoid using *hopefully* to mean "it is hoped": We *hoped* the pass would not be intercepted. *Not: Hopefully* the pass would not be intercepted.

if, whether To express doubt, use *whether:* They were uncertain *whether* the game would be telecast in their region. To express an alternative, use *whether or not: Whether or not* you can come, please call next week. Use *if* in an adverbial clause expressing a condition: *If* you can make it, we'd very much like to have you join us.

illicit See *elicit, illicit.*

illusion See *allusion, illusion.*

implicit See *explicit, implicit.*

imply, infer *Imply* means "to suggest"; *infer* means "to interpret or make a guess based on evidence." Readers *infer* what writers *imply*.

in, into, in to *In* suggests a stationary place or position; *into* indicates movement toward a place or position. While she was *in* the pool, the phone rang. When he dived *into* the pool, he made a terrific splash. Use *in to* when *to* is part of an infinitive: She went *in to* answer the phone.

irregardless, regardless *Irregardless* is nonstandard for *regardless. Regardless* (not *irregardless*) of their political connections, they still had to obey the traffic laws.

its, it's Use *its* only as a possessive adjective: The cat licked *its* fur. Use *it's* to mean "it is" or "it has": *It's* only a ten-minute walk. *It's* been raining steadily.

kind of, sort of Both expressions are informal for "rather." You may use them in formal writing, if *kind* and *sort* function as nouns: The panda is related to the raccoon; it is not a *kind of* bear. Avoid informal usages like the following in college writing: It was *kind of* an intriguing explanation. Instead write: It was an intriguing explanation.

lay, lie *Lie* means "to recline"; *lay* means "to put or place." I wanted to *lie* down and take a nap. Please *lay* the eyeglass case on the bookcase.

leave, let *Leave* means "to depart from" or "to let remain": She had to *leave* early. *Let* means "to allow to" or "to permit": The instructor *let* the class go early.

less, fewer See *fewer, less.*

lie, lay See *lay, lie.*

like See *as, like.*

lose, loose *Lose* is a verb with many meanings, including "to suffer defeat": I hope our team doesn't *lose* the game. *Loose* is usually an adjective, meaning "not firmly attached": This knot is too *loose*. As a verb *loose* means "to set free": They *loosed* the hounds for the foxhunt.

may, can See *can, may.*

maybe, may be *Maybe* is an adverb meaning "perhaps"; *may be* is a verb. *Maybe* I'll travel this summer. It *may be* more difficult than you think.

number See *amount, number.*

OK, O.K., okay All of these are informal expressions suitable for conversation, but not for formal writing.

percent, percentage *Percent* suggests a specific figure; *percentage* is a more general term. The retention rate at Notre Dame is nearly 99 *percent*. A high *percentage* of college students are not graduated from the schools they attended as freshmen.

phenomena Plural of *phenomenon:* Certain ocean *phenomena* baffle biologists.

principal, principle *Principal* refers either to a sum of money or to the leader or head of an entity such as a school: They collected their interest each month but they left the *principal* untouched. The *principal* decided to hold an assembly to address disciplinary problems in the school. *Principle* means "a fundamental belief": They refused to comply as a matter of *principle.*

quotation, quote *Quotation* is a noun and *quote* is a verb. Former President Bush was *quoted* as saying, "Read my lips; no new taxes." It was a *quotation* that would haunt him during his unsuccessful campaign for reelection.

raise, rise *Raise* means "to lift": Please *raise* the shade. *Rise* means "to get up": I will *rise* tomorrow before 6 a.m.

real, really *Real* is an adjective; *really* is an adverb. Avoid using *real* to mean "very." The purchase they made was a *real* value. The dinner was *very* good. It was a *really* exciting game.

reason is because This is a redundant construction to be avoided. Use either *because* or the *reason . . . that* instead. The *reason* they couldn't come was *that* they had a prior commitment. They couldn't come *because* they had a prior commitment. *Not:* The reason they couldn't come was because they had a prior commitment.

respectively, respectfully *Respectively* means "in the order given." *Respectfully* means "with respect." Alpha and omega are, *respectively*, the first and last letters of the Greek alphabet. The children behaved *respectfully* in the presence of their family's guests.

rise See *raise, rise*.

set, sit *Set* means "to put or place": Would you *set* this cup on the counter? *Sit* means to "seat oneself": May I *sit* on this antique chair?

should of Use *should have*. We *should have* avoided the freeway at rush hour.

sight, site See *cite, sight, site*.

sometime, some time, sometimes *Sometime* means "at an indefinite future time": We will get around to seeing them *sometime*. *Some time* means "a period of time": We would like to spend *some time* with them on our next vacation. *Sometimes* means "occasionally": *Sometimes* I lose my concentration.

sure, surely *Sure* is an adjective; *surely* is an adverb. She was *sure* of one thing at least. *Surely*, you have made a mistake. Avoid using *sure* as an intensifier or as an adverb in formal writing. Not: She was *sure* clever. Or: *Sure*, I agree. (Though such usage is fine in conversation.)

than, then The conjunction *than* is used in comparisons; the adverb *then* indicates time. Throughout the 1980s, the Mets had a better baseball team *than* the Yankees. *Then* in the next decade, things changed.

that, which, who *That*, *which*, and *who* are all relative pronouns. Use *that* to refer to things or people, *which* to refer only to things, and *who* to refer only to people. For his thirtieth birthday, she bought him the gift *that* he had not wanted to buy for himself. The opportunity, *which* will not readily come again, must not be passed by. Among the many attendees were some *who* couldn't wait to leave.

their, there, they're *Their* is a possessive pronoun; *there* is an adverb indicating place and is used in the common expressions "there is" and "there are"; *they're* is a contraction meaning "they are." When George Eliot and Jane Austen wrote *their* great novels, *there* were few creative opportunities for women, besides writing. Please put the books over *there*. *They're* unable to come until after the game begins.

then See *than, then*.

to, too, two *To* is a preposition; *too* means "also" or "excessively"; *two* is a number. The quarterback faked a handoff *to* the fullback and threw over the middle *to* the tight end. You *too* may one day enjoy a chance to travel. You ate *too* much and you ate *too* fast. You'd better take *two* antacids.

toward, towards Both are acceptable.

uninterested See *disinterested, uninterested*.

unique *Unique* means "the only one of its kind." Avoid using modifiers or intensifiers with *unique*. "Very unique" or "the most unique" are meaningless expressions.

use, utilize *Utilize* means "to put to use." Avoid the term *utilize* when *use* will convey your meaning equally well. The mayor urged city residents and commuters to *use* (not *utilize*) public transportation during the week of the festival.

well See *good, well*.

whether, if See *if, whether*.

which, that Although *which* may be used before both restrictive and nonrestrictive clauses, many writers prefer to use it only with nonrestrictive clauses containing nonessential information: The car, *which* was parked behind the house, had been badly damaged. (The essential point here is that the car had been badly damaged. Where it was parked is not as important.) *That* is used only with restrictive clauses: The car *that* was parked behind the house had been badly damaged. (In this case where the car was parked is essential information identifying which car had been badly damaged: that is, the car parked behind the house.)

who, whom Use *who* when a sentence requires a subject pronoun: *Who* will be able to come? Use *whom* when a sentence requires an object pronoun: *Whom* did you tell? In most instances, for relative clauses, use *who* before a verb: Mariela, *who* is Danish, speaks four languages. Before a noun or pronoun, use *whom:* Mariela, *whom* I have just met, speaks four languages.

whose, who's *Whose* is a possessive adjective; *who's* is a contraction meaning "who is." *Whose* umbrella is this? *Who's* responsible for this wonderful dessert?

your, you're *Your* is a possessive adjective; *you're* is a contraction for "you are." *Your* idea was well received by the committee. *You're* one of the most courageous people I've ever met.

Glossary of Terms

This glossary lists and defines selected grammatical terms used throughout *The Scribner Essentials for Writers*. For fuller explanations of terms and additional examples, see the relevant sections cited within most definitions.

absolute phrase A group of words often consisting of a participle and its subject. An absolute phrase modifies an independent clause as a whole. *The game over,* the team left the field. See p. 120.

active voice The verb form in which the grammatical subject is the agent and the direct object is the receiver of the verb's action. See p. 79. See also *passive voice.*

adjective A word that modifies a noun or pronoun: a *bright* light. See p. 89.

adjective clause A clause modifying a noun or pronoun in another clause. See p. 118.

adverb A word that modifies a verb, an adjective, or another adverb: *quickly, now.* See p. 89.

adverb clause A clause that modifies a verb, adjective, another adverb, or an entire sentence. See p. 118.

agreement Correspondence of a verb with its subject in person and number, and of a pronoun with its antecedent in number and gender. See *subject–verb agreement,* p. 79; and *pronoun–antecedent agreement,* p. 87.

antecedent The noun that a pronoun refers to: Bill and *his* friends. See p. 83.

appositive A noun, noun phrase, or pronoun that renames the noun or pronoun it immediately follows: my favorite day, *Saturday.* See p. 85.

article A type of determiner that precedes a noun: *a, an,* or *the.* See p. 95.

auxiliary verb Also called a *helping verb,* an auxiliary verb combines with a main verb to form a complete verb or verb phrase: We *will* attend. See pp. 72 and 100.

case The changes in form a noun or pronoun undergoes to indicate whether it functions as subject, object, or possessor: *they, them, their; Tom, Tom's.* See p. 83.

clause A group of words that contains a subject and a predicate. See p. 118. See also *dependent clause; independent clause.*

collective noun A noun that names a group of people or things: *team, family, committee.* See p. 81.

comma splice Two independent clauses incorrectly separated by a comma instead of a period. See p. 93.

complement A word or group of words that completes the meaning of a subject or a direct object by renaming or describing it.

complex sentence A single independent clause with one or more dependent clauses.

compound-complex sentence Two or more independent clauses and at least one dependent clause.

compound sentence Two or more independent clauses joined by a coordinating conjunction, without any dependent clauses.

compound subject Two or more simple subjects joined by a coordinating or correlative conjunction. See p. 80.

conjunction A word that links words, phrases, and clauses to one another: *bread and butter.*

conjunctive adverb An adverb that emphasizes the relationship in meaning between two independent clauses: *therefore, however.*

coordinating conjunction A conjunction that joins words and phrases as well as independent clauses: *and, but, or, nor, for, so,* and *yet.* See p. 116.

correlative conjunction A paired conjunction that links words, phrases, and clauses: *both . . . and.*

count noun A noun that can be counted and can take both a plural and singular form: *acorns, oaks, pens.* See p. 95.

demonstrative pronoun A pronoun that points to a particular thing: *This* is an ugly poster; *those* are useless flyers.

dependent clause A group of words that begins with a relative pronoun or a subordinating conjunction: *before the game begins.* A dependent clause has both a subject and a verb but cannot stand alone as a sentence. See p. 92.

direct object A noun or pronoun that receives the action of a transitive verb in a sentence. See p. 72. See also *indirect object.*

ellipses Three equally spaced dots signifying that words have been omitted from a quotation: *And I have miles . . . before I sleep.* See p. 133.

expletive A construction that begins with the word *here*, *there*, or *it* and is followed by a form of the verb *to be: There is* an expletive in this sentence.

gerund A verbal ending in *-ing* that functions as a noun in a sentence: *Smoking* is prohibited.

gerund phrase A group of words consisting of a gerund with related modifiers, objects, or complements.

helping verb An auxiliary verb that accompanies the main verb in a sentence: We *were* driving. See p. 100.

indefinite pronoun A pronoun that refers to an unspecified person (*somebody*) or thing (*anything*). See pp. 80 and 88.

independent clause A group of words consisting of a subject and a predicate. An independent clause can stand alone as a sentence. See p. 92.

indirect object A noun or pronoun that indicates *to whom* or *for whom* the action of a verb in a sentence is performed. See also *direct object*.

infinitive In the present, a verbal consisting of the base form of the verb and *to* (*to win*); in the past, a verbal that includes *to*, the past participle of *have*, and the past participle of the verb (*to have won*). Infinitives can function as nouns, adjectives, or adverbs.

infinitive phrase A group of words consisting of an infinitive with its related modifiers, objects, or complements. Infinitive phrases can function as nouns, adjectives, or adverbs.

intensive pronoun A *-self* form of pronoun that emphasizes its antecedent: *yourself.*

interjection An emphatic word or phrase that expresses surprise or emotion: *Wow!* or *Hey!*

interrogative pronoun A pronoun that introduces a question (*who, which, what*). See p. 84.

intransitive verb A verb that does not take a direct object: The whistle *blew*. See p. 72. See also *transitive verb*.

irregular verb A verb that forms the past tense and past participle in ways other than adding *-d, -ed*, or *-t*: *begin, began, begun*. See p. 73.

linking verb A verb that joins the subject of a sentence to a subject complement. Linking verbs indicate conditions, states of being, or sense experience: It *will* rain; He *was* tired; They *are* cold. See p. 73.

main clause See *independent clause.*

modal auxiliary verbs Also called *modals.* Combine with main verbs to indicate necessity (*must*), obligation (*should, ought*), permission (*may*), or possibility (*might*). See p. 103.

modifier A word or phrase that functions as an adjective or adverb to limit or qualify the meaning of a word, phrase, or clause. See pp. 90–91.

mood A writer's or speaker's attitude indicated by a verb's action, whether imperative, indicative, or subjunctive. See p. 78.

noun Names a person, place, thing, concept, or quality. Nouns can be common (*disk*), proper (*Sharon*), abstract (*innocence*), concrete (*ketchup*), collective (*class*), or mass (*weather*).

noun clause A clause that typically begins with a relative pronoun and functions as a subject, an object, or a complement in a sentence.

object A word or group of words, functioning as a noun or pronoun, that is influenced by a verb (direct object), a verbal (indirect object), or a preposition (object of a preposition). See p. 72.

object complement A noun or adjective that follows a direct object and describes or renames it.

object of a preposition A noun or pronoun that follows a preposition and completes its meaning.

parallelism The use of a similar grammatical form for two or more coordinate words, phrases, or clauses to achieve clarity, elegance, or equivalence.

participial phrase A group of words consisting of a present or past participle and accompanying modifiers, objects, or complements that functions as an adjective.

participle A verbal that functions as an adjective. Present participles end in *-ing* (*burning*); past participles of regular verbs end in *-d* or *-ed* (*burned*). See p. 98.

parts of speech The categories into which words are grouped according to their grammatical function in sentences: verbs, nouns, pronouns, adjectives, adverbs, prepositions, conjunctions, and interjections.

passive voice The verb form in which the grammatical subject receives the verb's action, rather than directing that action as in the *active voice.* See pp. 79 and 102. See also *active voice.*

past participle The third principal part of the verb that includes qualities of both an adjective and a verb. The past participle usually ends in *-d* or *-ed*. See p. 98.

personal pronoun A pronoun that refers to a person or a thing: *we, you, they, him, her, it*. See p. 84.

phrase A group of related words that does not form a complete sentence and that functions as a noun, verb, or modifier. See p. 92.

possessive case Indicates when a pronoun shows ownership: *your, yours*. See p. 84.

predicate The part of a sentence containing the finite verb. The predicate describes what the subject is doing or experiencing or what is being done to the subject: The car *rolled*; We *were asleep*.

preposition A word that indicates the relationship between a noun or pronoun and other words in a sentence.

prepositional phrase A group of words consisting of a preposition, its object, and any of the object's modifiers. Prepositional phrases function as adjectives or adverbs.

present participle The *-ing* form of the verb, which functions as an adjective: *sewing, speaking*. See p. 98.

pronoun A word that takes the place of a noun. See p. 83.

reflexive pronoun A *-self* form of the pronoun that refers to the subject of the clause in which it appears.

regular verb A verb that forms its past tense and past participle by adding *-d* or *-ed* (or in some cases *-t*) to the base form. See p. 72.

relative clause A clause introduced by a relative pronoun.

relative pronoun A pronoun that introduces a clause that modifies a noun or pronoun: *who, which, that*. See pp. 84 and 93.

restrictive clause A clause serving as an adjective or adverb that limits or restricts the meaning of the word(s) modified. See p. 117.

sentence A group of words that includes a subject and a predicate. A sentence begins with a capital letter and ends with a mark of end punctuation.

sentence fragment A group of words that begins with a capital letter and ends with end punctuation but is grammatically incomplete. See p. 92.

simple sentence A single independent clause.

subject The grammatical part of a sentence indicating what it is about.

subject complement A noun or adjective that follows a linking verb and identifies or describes the subject of the sentence.

subjunctive mood The mood of a verb expressing wishes, stipulating demands or requirements, or making statements contrary to fact: I wish I *were* rich. See p. 78.

subordinate clause See *dependent clause.*

subordinating conjunction A conjunction that introduces a dependent (or subordinate) clause indicating the relationship of the dependent clause to the main or independent clause of a sentence.

tense The time of a verb's action or state of being, such as past, present, and future. See p. 76.

transitive verb A verb that takes a direct object: He *washed* the car. See p. 72. See also *intransitive verb.*

verb A part of the predicate of a sentence that describes an action or occurrence or indicates a state of being. Verbs change form to indicate tense, voice, mood, person, or number. See Chapter 20.

verbal A verb form that functions as a noun or a modifier rather than as a verb in a sentence. Verbals may be infinitives, present or past participles, and gerunds.

Index

175

Topic/Thesis

- ☐ Is my topic well focused?
- ☐ Does my thesis statement identify my topic and make an assertion about it?
- ☐ Is my thesis statement positioned so that readers will not miss it?

Purpose/Organization

- ☐ Is my purpose clear? Is my organizational pattern suited to my purpose?
- ☐ Is my organizational pattern easy for my readers to follow?
- ☐ Is the logic of my argument sound?

Paragraphs

- ☐ Are my paragraphs unified, well-developed, and coherent?
- ☐ Do my topic sentences relate to my thesis? Do they support my thesis?

Sentences/Diction

- ☐ Do my sentences convey my thoughts clearly?
- ☐ Do my sentences emphasize the most important aspects of each thought?
- ☐ Is the structure of my sentences varied?
- ☐ Do I engage my reader with concrete nouns and strong action verbs?
- ☐ Do I use appropriate language given my subject and my audience?

Documentation of Sources

- ☐ Is borrowed material introduced by a signal phrase and documented with a parenthetical in-text citation?
- ☐ Have I properly documented all material that is not common knowledge?
- ☐ Are my direct quotations accurate and enclosed within quotation marks or set off in block format?
- ☐ Is my paper free of plagiarism? Have I used my own words and sentence structure for summaries and paraphrases?

REVISION SYMBOLS

Boldface numbers and letters refer to
Essentials chapters and sections.

ab	abbreviation **37**		¶ dev	paragraph development needed
ad	form of adjective/ adverb **22**		¶ type	paragraph type inappropriate
agr	agreement **20f, 21d**		prep	inappropriate preposition
awk	awkward diction or construction **24c**		pron	incorrect pronoun form **21**
bias	biased language **27c, d**		ref	unclear pronoun reference **21**
ca	case **21a, b**			
cap	capitalization **36**		rep	unnecessary repetition
coh	coherence		search	check research or citation **7–12**
coord	coordination			
cs	comma splice **23b**		sp	spelling error
d	diction, word choice **27**		shift	inconsistent, shifted construction
dm	dangling modifier **22e**		sub	sentence subordination
dev	development needed **13–15; 41–42**		t	verb tense error **20c**
			trans	transition needed
doc	check documentation **16–19**		var	sentence variety needed **28**
emph	emphasis needed **26**		vb	verb form error **20**
frag	sentence fragment **23a**		w	wordy **25, 27**
fs	fused sentence **23b**		ww/wc	wrong word; word choice **24, 27a**
hyph	hyphen **40**			
idea dev	develop ideas, thinking, or reading **1–6**		//	faulty parallelism **29**
int m	interrupting modifier **22d**		. ? !	end punctuation **35a, b, c**
inc	incomplete construction **29**		:	colon **32**
			'	apostrophe **33**
ital	italics **39**		—	dash **35d**
k	awkward diction or construction **24c**		( )	parentheses **35e**
lc	lower-case letter **36**		[ ]	brackets **35f**
log	logic		. . .	ellipses **35h**
mm	misplaced modifier **22d**		/	slash **35g**
ms	manuscript form **16–19; 41–42**		:	semicolon **31**
			" "	quotation marks **34**
mix	mixed construction **29**		⌢	comma **30**
no ¶	no paragraph needed			close up
			∧	insert a missing element
num	number **38**		↲	delete
¶	paragraph		∿	transpose order

Contents

186

Part 3

Researching: Documenting Sources   29

Part 4

Grammar   71

Part 5

Style   *105*

Part 6

Punctuation and Mechanics   *115*